# THRIVI TRUTH

## Freedom for Intimidators
## and Victims

**Dan Chesney**

# Thriving On Truth

## Freedom for Intimidators and Victims

Dan Chesney

New Wine Press

New Wine Press
PO Box 17
Chichester PO20 6YB
England

Unless otherwise stated Bible quotations are taken from the NKJV
New King James Bible, © 1984 Thomas Nelson Inc, Nashville, USA

ISBN 1 874367 21 3

Typeset by CRB (Drayton) Typesetting Services, Drayton, Norwich
Printed in England by Clays Ltd, St Ives plc.

This book is dedicated to all those who are seeking to walk in the light, who daily face difficult relationships but still desire to change. May God give them grace, courage and faith to scale seemingly impossible mountains and to shout from the top, 'All things are possible to those who believe!'

Special thanks to Annette Callaway who faithfully helped get this book to the publishers in spite of her two-year-old son running circles around her computer. Your dedication is deeply appreciated.

# Preface

The relationships and circumstances in which we find ourselves often become our watershed. The grass would be so much greener if it were not for difficult people and overpowering situations. Who wants to be a victim? Who wants to live under an intimidating, controlling, manipulative person? Who likes to think of himself as a domineering ogre?

This book is about the possibilities for real change in the human character and personality. The tough issues of victim and victor, master and slave, intimidator and intimidatee are discussed frankly. And real answers, God's answers, are brought to light to help bring the grace and redemptive power of Christ into relationships. *Thriving On Truth* pulls no punches. The victim's mentality and intimidation tactics are unveiled in the face of truth and God's process for healing.

You do not have to remain stuck in unloving, unfulfilling relationships. Christ came and demonstrated the answer. Jesus was radical in His relationships. If you are willing to be confronted with the truth and start living in peace, then this book is for you.

When Jesus stepped into history He broke the cycle of

sin. Now He desires to step into your relationships and personality to break the cycle of unwanted behavioural patterns. Jesus offers healthy, loving ways to build relationships and face life. This book is a step along that journey of freedom and wholeness.

# Contents

**PART III: Who is Winning – Victim or Victor?**

**PART IV: Stepping Into Freedom**

# PART I

## Victorious Victims

# Facing the Truth

Overcoming a victim mentality begins with facing the truth. Ted Armstrong, in speaking to leaders, said, 'Real change and emotional growth come when we face our weaknesses and personality defects and take seriously the criticism levelled at us by friends and foes alike.'[1] We may often feel victimized by our circumstances, other people or even by our own decisions, but by facing the truth in each incident God can bring possibilities of good and hope out of them all.

The good news that Jesus brings to us is that we do not have to remain the way we are. As was said of Saul, '...*God gave him another heart*...',[2] or turned him into another man. This is what this book is about, helping people see that being changed into another person can become a present tense reality as they learn to thrive on truth.

1.  *Seizing the Torch* by Ted W. Armstrong and Robert C. Larson – Regal Books
2.  1 Samuel 10:9 (NKJV)

# *Chapter 1*

## Moses' Freedom From Co-dependency

'Moses, don't you dare touch our baby boy, or I will use
that knife to circumcise your brain.' Moses looked over at
his wife and could see her eyes watching every move he
made. Though she was still a little weak from the birth of
their son Gershom, he knew that her temper was more
than he wanted to tangle with now.

'Yes dear, we will talk about circumcision later. I know
it is not the custom of your people.' Moses felt it was
better to just leave the tent until his wife Zipporah calmed
down. Her motherly instincts were working overtime.
There would be another day.

Moses had a significant encounter with God in Egypt.
He was converted and called to bring deliverance to millions of Jews – a large vision by anybody's standards.
However, in zealous, misguided faith, Moses murdered a
man. He thought that was God's will and way of bringing
deliverance.

His crime was soon discovered and he had to flee. God
then gave him forty years to think about his methods. To
help pass the time in his new occupation of shepherding,
he married Zipporah. They then had a son, and on the
eighth day after this wonderful event, Moses told his wife
it was time to circumcise Gershom. Zipporah did not like

the idea of Moses cutting up their baby boy. So they had an argument which Zipporah apparently won. As a good husband, Moses decided it was easier to keep the peace than to be the target of his wife's tongue. A second son was born, and Moses probably decided not to say anything because he still remembered the last episode.

Many years later God appeared to Moses and renewed his call to deliver Israel. After some reluctance and much persuasion, Moses had to face the most powerful and evil man in the world – Pharaoh. But on the way to this encounter we read:

> *'At a lodging place on the way, the Lord met Moses and was about to kill him. But Zipporah took a flint knife, cut off her son's foreskin and touched Moses' feet with it. "Surely you are a bridegroom of blood to me," she said. So the Lord let him alone. (At that time she said "bridegroom of blood," referring to circumcision).'*[1]

God was bringing up an old family dispute, one Moses had been avoiding for years. God would no longer permit this issue to remain hidden. Moses compromised God's command to circumcise his children in order to appease his wife. Now God was asking him to make the choice. God would not allow revival for the nation of Israel until **Moses faced his wife**. Moses was willing to face Egypt, Pharaoh, Israel, even God, but he was afraid of his own intimidating wife.

## Confronted with Truth

God's love and light confronted Moses. He had to make the choice. Was he going to obey his wife or God? What looked on the surface like a loving thing to do was in reality disobedience. Yes, Moses had some seemingly good reasons for not circumcising his son. His wife had just had a baby. She was tired and emotionally very protective of her child. Circumcision was not the custom of his wife's people. Maybe they had not talked about it beforehand. There are always plausible reasons, but are they compromising our obedience to Christ?

God knew that if Moses did not face his wife's intimidation, it would be like a cancer that would spread. God was calling for obedience in **all areas**. Moses could no longer think of himself as a victim, or even as a gracious, loving husband. God called it what it was – unbelief and disobedience. Imagine, a whole nation's deliverance depended upon Moses facing his intimidator – his own wife. Prayer was not going to work, fasting could not be a substitute. He had to face her.

I know of another marriage where the husband is a dominating, selfish, demanding man, and the wife is an acquiescing, smiling servant. She is a Christian and he is not. Slowly over the years he has attempted every trick of manipulation, threats and verbal lashing to restrict her Christian life. He is a hypochondriac who demands her constant attention for one physical ailment after another. Furthermore he regularly threatens to cut her off financially if she does not submit to him.

Over the years she has slowly convinced herself that it is God's will to submit to his demands. She has forfeited church life, isolated herself from Christian friends, and has highly restricted her personal devotional life.

From outward appearances she looks like Florence Nightingale, but in reality she has compromised for personal gain. She remains well supported financially but could lose it all if she ever faces up to him. Her loving graciousness is a mask for insecurities and unbelief. She has subtly transferred her faith from God to her husband. In this way the husband is never confronted with his sin and she never has to face her sin.

This is co-dependency: two people in a relationship who are over-dependent upon each other. The statement these kind of relationships make is, 'I will change if and when the other person changes.' But of course the other person does not change. That is why God had to force the issue with Moses; Zipporah's views never did change.

This mutual unchangeableness is what keeps each person in psychological and emotional bondage. An even deeper bondage which most counsellors never deal with is that of spiritual bondage.

God calls us to change, to believe Him regardless of people, circumstances or our personal past history. God expected Saul to obey and believe regardless of the people's demands. Jesus expected Peter to walk on the water regardless of the storm. Then when both of these men failed, Jesus exposed the reason that they yielded to the intimidation; it was unbelief.

Moses wanted his wife to see the light regarding circumcision. He just did not want to be the one to tell her. Saul desired to obey Samuel's word, but he also could not bring himself to explain it to his people. Peter deeply aspired to walk on the water. He just felt that now was not the best time to do it. And this wife longed for her husband to be saved, but instead she was falling more and more under his dominion, just as Moses fell under his wife, Saul under his people and Peter under the water.

This wife had deceived herself into thinking that her husband would get saved through her longsuffering, which in actuality was a guise for compromise. As long as truth is compromised, salvation cannot happen. Jesus said, *'And you shall **know** the **truth**, and the **truth** shall make you free.'*[2] She had been avoiding the truth because she was afraid not just of his anger, but of losing what she had. This is not living in faith but in fear. Her co-dependency brought her into spiritual bondage – she was believing a lie.

Jesus was the greatest example of love, yet He never compromised the truth when He was faced with intimidation of the Pharisees, His disciples, His family or His situation. He always obeyed His Father. And this is to be the standard for us also in loving other people.

## Right and Wrong Suffering

The wife in our example was confused as to why Jesus died and suffered for her. Malcolm Smith said it well:

'If Jesus had died to help people, it would have been pointless, a wasted heap of ashes; but, because he died at the Father's command, He was exalted to be their Saviour and **rescuer**. Likewise, Christians are called to obey God, not to go around laying down their lives for everyone who asks them to, ending up on the ash heap and whimpering that no-one cares.'[3]

She was laying her life down for self-fulfilment, not because Jesus commanded it.

The apostle Peter tells us to endure sufferings and wrongs committed toward us if we are in a situation beyond our control such as prisoners of war or living in a country of dictatorship. Yet in all our suffering of wrong, we are still never to compromise the truth, even if it means we are to die for it. Peter said,

> *'In this you greatly rejoice, though now for a little while, if need be, you have been grieved by various trials, that the genuineness of your faith, being much more precious than gold that perishes, though it is tested by fire, may be found to praise, honour and glory at the revelation of Jesus Christ, whom having not seen you love. Though now you do not see Him, yet believing, you rejoice with joy inexpressible and full of glory.'*[4]

Suffering here is endured with great rejoicing; *'joy inexpressible and full of glory.'*[4] All true suffering for Christ's sake is accompanied by joy. Yet most women, who like this lady are living under the constant spirit of fear and intimidation, are not leaping for joy. This is because it is a false submission, something which God is neither requiring of the individual nor giving them grace to endure. True suffering for Christ is not cowering in fear but trusting in God. Peter says, *'and do not be afraid of their threats, nor be troubled.'*[5] Paul says, *'...and not for a moment intimidated,'* or *'...never be scared for a second by your opponents.'*[6] Why? Because your fearlessness is a sign that they are wrong.

The sufferings that the New Testament writers talk about range from death to imprisonment, loss of material wealth to physical beatings. Yet in all of these the Christian is to remain full of joy and fearlessness. How? By faith in Christ and by living as the new person you are in Christ.

However, these are not the kinds of trials that are

found in the lives of most individuals such as this lady who was submitting to a dominating husband. And because she is not living in faith but in fear, depression and self-pity are the result.

Being married to an unsaved partner will bring persecution and trials, but **what** we submit to is crucial, as well as **why** we submit to it. Peter goes on to say that if we suffer for doing **good** we are blessed. But doing **good** is not cowering to intimidation or compromising because of threats and living in anger. That is playing into the Devil's hands.

Peter says,

> '...*having a good conscience, that when they defame you as evildoers, those who revile your **good conduct** in Christ may be ashamed. For it is better, if it is the will of God, to suffer for doing **good** than for doing evil.*'[7]

And what is this **good conduct** for which we may suffer? Obeying Christ **first**, holy living, speaking the truth, rejoicing always, trusting God.

Like this wife, many people compromise and become silent sufferers in order to live as comfortably as possible. This lady knew that if she deepened her devotion to Christ it would bring out more of the beast than was already apparent in her husband, and that was the price she was not willing to pay. Then she would be suffering for righteousness sake. But instead she is experiencing the pain for compromise.

> '*For Christ also suffered once for sins, the just for the unjust, that He might bring us to God, being put to death in the flesh but made alive by the Spirit.*'[8]

This is the key. True suffering brings death to self but life in our hearts. Compromise brings a saving of self and quenches our spiritual life.

Now I need to make a statement to prevent any wrong thinking which may be developing. I am not advocating that all brow-beaten wives, henpecked husbands, victimized teenagers or oppressed people who are living under the tyranny of fear and intimidation, should rise up in rebellious rage and storm their intimidator with a flag saying, 'I have rights!' That would only be another display of self. What I am saying is that Christ's glory must be revealed as the victim rises up in faith in God and right living in Christ. This will threaten the intimidator more than anything else because he/she will see that his/her victim is no longer under his/her control but rather rejoicing in Christ.

It is no wonder that the feminist movement has sprung up. It is a reaction to male chauvinism. But the end does not justify the means. The spirit and motive of the whole feminist movement is wrong. Feminists are attempting to throw off all restraints to promote female 'selfism'.

There are times when confrontation is right, when the language of love is strong and the intimidator must be faced. However, more often than not the intimidator is not the problem – we are! It is our fears, our doubts, our insecurities, our weaknesses that need to be exposed. Facing our intimidator is facing ourselves. And it is at this moment of honesty that the Holy Spirit can begin to change us into the image of Christ.

Being a loving wife to a domineering husband, or a loving person in any relationship involving a dominant individual, does not mean becoming a doormat. Wives are to win their unsaved husbands to Christ by their godly cónduct, and that conduct is living the truth out before them.

This means that both the intimidator and the intimidatee need to repent because both are attempting to win through self effort. They have not learned the biblical meaning of, '... *reckon yourselves to be dead indeed unto sin...*'9 Both are walking in the flesh and not in the Spirit. Both Moses and Zipporah had to change, both had to repent, both had to obey God.

## Footnotes

1. Exodus 4:24–26 (NIV)
2. John 8:32 (NKJV)
3. *Toxic Love*, Malcolm Smith, Pillar Books & Publishing
4. 1 Peter 1:6–8 (NKJV)
5. 1 Peter 3:14 (NKJV)
6. Philippians 1:28 (Moffat)
7. 1 Peter 3:16–17 (NKJV)
8. 1 Peter 3:18 (NKJV)
9. Romans 6:11 (NKJV)

## *Chapter 2*

## Gideon – The Angry Young Man

'The Midianites! Every time I think of them my blood runs cold. Why did Abraham ever marry Keturah after Sarah died? It has only lead to oppression by their son Midian.'

'You are right, Gideon,' cried a fellow Israelite. 'He should have quit when he was ahead, at least Isaac was a peaceful man.'

These remarks only stirred the fury in Gideon's heart: 'It has been seven years now that these Midianites and Amalekites, (and who knows how many other 'ites' there will be), have been raping our land. They steal our live-stock, trample our crops and abuse our women. These Easterners ... these nomadic parasites, have impoverished our land. Look at us! We are hiding like goats in a cave.'

Another voice emerged from among all the vigorous affirmation saying, 'We have vented our anger a thousand times before. We have prayed to...'

'Do not say His name. You will only bring more curses on us.'

Suddenly all eyes turned towards the new voice that came from the crude doorway made of tightly woven branches, a substitute for the fine doors Israel once enjoyed in their times of prosperity under Joshua. It was Joash the Abiezrite, Gideon's father.

'Gideon, we need you at home. It is time to thresh the wheat. Maybe we can beat those detestable invaders this year and enjoy some bread.'

As Gideon reluctantly rose, his anger slowly boiled into depression. He was not in the mood to work so hard, only to have all the wheat so neatly prepared for the war-mongers. 'How could Yahweh have abandoned us after all He did for our forefathers, after all the promises He made to us through Abraham, Isaac, Jacob and Moses?' Just the thought rekindled his sense of injustice. His youthful lips could not restrain his emotions and he muttered in disgust, 'I will see Israel avenged, even if I have to do it myself.'

Gideon was an angry man, and for legitimate reasons. Israel was devastated year after year by the Midianites and Amalekites. They were so numerous and their ravage so extensive that they were compared to swarms of locusts.

He had lived under their tyranny long enough. But, like all the other Israelites, he was too intimidated to lead a resistance against them. Gideon knew what it felt like to be intimidated. He not only had to endure that cursed state of helplessness, but he could see the effects of it in his family and his country.

What did he see that distressed him the most? It was not the loss of property (even though that had created an enormous homeless problem), nor was it the prospect of spending another winter season scratching for food. It was the idols. As angry as he was at the invaders, and at Yahweh for allowing it all to happen, Gideon was more ashamed that his own people worshipped the gods of the Ammonites. He saw a people of compromise. In his heart he knew this compromise was nothing less than negotiating with the Devil for a little more time to do things their way rather than Yahweh's way.

In the two unbalanced relationships that we have looked at so far, both people know they are wrong, but both compromise so that self can remain alive. And as long as conditions are tolerable, meaning as long as self is still getting its way, both individuals are willing to live with the situation. But, like Gideon, there is a cost to our indulgence of idols, whether they be idols of self-pity, fear, machismo or the Ammonite gods.

There is a clear example of this in 1 Samuel chapter 11 when Nahash the Ammonite came up against Jabesh Gilead. The people of Jabesh Gilead were frightened and intimidated by the force of the Ammonites. In their fear their first concern was to save themselves, their **self-life**. They did not act in faith. They did not call upon the name of the Lord. Instead they sought a compromise. They said, *'Make a covenant with us, and we will serve you.'*[1] In other words, let us live, let us have a little freedom and allow our lives to go on as normal, and then we will bow to your intimidation.

The Ammonites loved this. They were winning through intimidation without even a battle. But there was the catch, the price of compromise, the bondage:

> *'On this condition* (a key word) *I will make a covenant with you, that I may put out all your right eyes, and bring reproach on all Israel.'*[2]

Intimidators always seek to bring reproach on their

victims. It makes them feel superior. This reproach frightened the elders of Jabesh to such an extent that they sent out a cry for help. And how did God deliver them? The Spirit of the Lord rose up in righteous anger in Saul who then **confronted** the intimidators. Saul went and faced the Ammonites in the power of the Lord and brought deliverance to the people of Jabesh.

## Gideon's Moment of Truth

Gideon was going to have to confront the Midianites, but he knew he could not do it alone. Most people who feel afraid find themselves to be in this same position. They feel alone. They would like a Saul to come along and rescue them but they are cut off, at least in their thinking. They have forgotten God.

Gideon got the shock of his life when God showed up at his farm and said, *'The Lord is **with you**, you mighty man of valour!'*[3] Number one, Gideon did not know God was with him in such a personal way, and number two, Gideon would never have imagined that he was a valiant man, a hero!

When a person lives under intimidation for any length of time, he loses touch with who he really is. He is convinced that he is what his intimidator tells him he is, or what his situation says to him.

Living in fear keeps him in the soul realm. He is always conscious of what his emotional and psychological conditions are. Simultaneously this way of living deadens the person to his own spiritual life. This is why people believe their situation or their intimidator more than God's Word. Their minds tell them, 'You will never escape.' 'You deserve this.' 'God does not love you, or else He would help you.' Over and over the thoughts of the intim-idator and the lies of the Devil cascade through their minds like a torrential waterfall.

Our emotions only confirm our thoughts as we feel so worthless, stupid, unqualified and undeserving. Fear and anger, guilt and shame fluctuate by the hour until we are too tired to fight back.

All this takes place in the soul, and as long as we live there we are fighting a losing battle. Our power to live victoriously rests in the spirit realm. God empowers our inner person. And it is when we are in touch with Christ in our hearts that freedom begins.

Gideon said to the Lord, *'O my Lord, how can I save Israel? Indeed my clan is the weakest in Manasseh, and I am the least in my father's house.'*[4]

Is this not what the victim says: 'How can I save Israel? How can I truly love this person who treats me with such disrespect? How can I be free from fear? How can I live in joy and victory when this person is so dominating and controlling?'

Why did Gideon think that way? Even though God made a personal appearance to him, and told him in an audible voice that he was a mighty man of valour, Gideon **still did not believe God!** Why? He believed his emotions, his thoughts, his situation and his intimidating invaders **more than God's word**. Gideon was living in his soul realm and not walking in the Spirit.

The Lord was showing Gideon what he was really like, what his heart was like – a **mighty man of valour**. But Gideon had never seen that about himself. He had only seen himself as weak and insignificant. Gideon said to the Lord, *'Indeed my clan is the **weakest** in Manasseh, and I am the **least** in my father's house.'*[5]

God saw Gideon as a mighty man. Gideon saw himself as weak and insignificant. God was looking at his heart, Gideon was looking at his soul and circumstances. It was his wrong perception that kept him in the victim syndrome.

God was **already** with Gideon. Gideon was **already** a **mighty man**. Gideon was **already anointed to change history** in a nation. But Gideon was too busy listening to his thoughts, feeling his emotions and complaining about his situation to understand his full potential.

This is the great thing the intimidator dreads: the victim's realisation that he does not have to be a victim. It was this revelation which caused Gideon to defeat his oppressors and live in freedom.

So many people are believing the lie which holds them in bondage. Hear the word of the Lord:

You are not what your intimidator tells you you are.

You are not what your past history tells you you are.

You are not what the Devil tells you you are.

## Discovering Who You Are

You are what Christ has created you to be:

> *'Therefore, if anyone is in Christ, he is a new creation; old things have passed away; behold, all things have become new.'*[6]

Gideon finally saw the truth of what the Lord was saying. He was not what his emotions, his mind or his situation said he was – a scared, helpless man. He was what God had created him to be, 'a mighty man of valour.' Whatever we were, we are no longer in Christ. The old has gone, the new has come.

When I was young my father used to call me a name. It did not matter whether I was good or bad. It was used indiscriminately. When I would come home from school it was, 'Here comes the dummy.' At the table, out at play or just watching the telly, I would constantly hear 'Hey, dummy!' It was not long before I believed him. All through my school years I struggled with this image, never feeling I was quite good enough, smart enough, or successful enough. Even when I was in graduate school getting top marks, the image was always there.

Until, like Gideon, God broke that image. I was reading the Word one day when I came across 1 Corinthians 2:16: *'But we have the mind of Christ.'* I saw it, I was not a dummy, I was a genius! God's wisdom now flowed through my mind, I was not limited to my own intelligence. The mind of God was in me. This was already a fact, but I had not seen it. So with Gideon, the Lord had said to him, *'Go in this might of yours...'*[7] Gideon already had the anointing, the power. But he never availed himself of it. I too had not drawn upon the wisdom and creativity of God.

This is the devastating effect of living under intimidation and allowing other people to dominate you. You will never blossom into the full potential God has created for you. Ever since Adam and Eve the Devil has attemped to stamp mankind with his image, to try to destroy God's creation and distort it. Like Gideon, as we look over the fields of the world, we can see the mutations, distortions and perversions of life. All God created was **good**. Now His whole redemptive work through Christ and the Holy Spirit is to restore man back into the image of God.

And He has accomplished it. Our hearts have been *'...sprinkled from an evil conscience and our bodies washed with pure water.'*[8] *'For by one offering He has perfected forever those who are being sanctified.'*[9]

We no longer have to be slaves to our thoughts, our past, our images, our intimidators or our emotions. Christ's blood has washed us:

> *'How much more shall the blood of Christ, who through the eternal Spirit offered Himself without spot to God, purge* (cleanse) *your conscience from dead works to serve the living God?'*[10]

God has done a miracle in our hearts. The Living Bible says,

> *'For God took the sinless Christ and poured into Him our sins. Then, in exchange, He poured God's goodness into us!'*[11]

But this miracle has taken place in our hearts, our spirit, **not in our soul or body**. That is why God instructs us to walk in the Spirit and not in the flesh, because our inner person is the redeemed, sanctified, resurrected us. The **mighty man** was on the inside of Gideon, the **genius of God** was on the inside of me. And the **bold rejoicer** is on the inside of you.

Being free from your intimidator does not always mean breaking off the relationship, especially if it is family. But it does mean relating to your intimidator in an entirely **new way**. Gideon stopped being angry and started living in faith, believing who God said he was and not what was said by his intimidators, his emotions, his thoughts or his circumstances.

This is the essence of freedom. One might be in prison,

as was Paul, but he was a freer man than his jailers. When Paul stood before Felix and his accusers he said, *'This being so, I myself always strive to have a conscience without offense toward God and man.'*[12] The Roman Empire and the entire Jewish religious hierarchy were afraid of Paul, so they threatened him, beat him and imprisoned him in an attempt to stop him from preaching the Gospel. They used every intimidation tactic they knew. But Paul was truly a free man. He stood there with a pure conscience. Neither the circumstances nor the people determined who was free. It was his faith in God's Word which determined Paul's liberty.

## Footnotes

1. 1 Samuel 11:1 (NKJV)
2. 1 Samuel 11:2 (NKJV)
3. Judges 6:12 (NKJV)
4. Judges 6:15 (NKJV)
5. Judges 6:15 (NKJV)
6. 2 Corinthians 5:17 (NKJV)
7. Judges 6:14 (NKJV)
8. Hebrews 10:22 (NKJV)
9. Hebrews 10:14 (NKJV)
10. Hebrews 9:14 (NKJV)
11. 2 Corinthians 5:21 (LB)
12. Acts 24:16 (NKJV)

# Chapter 3

## Winning Over Fear, Intimidation and Co-dependency

Everybody is into winning, which is why a book called *Winning Through Intimidation* stormed the market as a best seller a number of years ago. If Zipporah and the Midianites were alive today, they could have been the authors. The question is, how and why do we want to win? Jesus won our victory so that He could give. Satan desires to win so that he can control. *Winning Through Intimidation* was a best seller within the business world because managers, salesmen and executives wanted a method by which they could get the upper hand.

Intimidation is just one method of frightening people into submission and gaining control over other people's lives. Intimidation is used to promote self and degrade others. It plays on people's fears, insecurities and poor self-image. It brings individuals into bondage and reproduces the oldest game known to man – master and slave.

How do people intimidate? By yelling, having a better education, using bigger words, giving stares that could kill, silence, threats, innuendoes, showing themselves as superior, using physical strength, blackmail, psychological mind games, and the list goes on...

Jesus came to break the power of hell in our lives, to set

us free from fear and intimidation. So many people cower
when their buttons are pressed. Moses ran from trouble in
Egypt, so when Zipporah rose up in anger he did not want
a repeat play. His button of insecurity was pushed and he
backed down. We do not want to keep responding the
same way to someone's anger or gifted use of language,
but every time it happens we find ourselves giving in or
backing off. Even though we know the other person is
wrong, we still accept their way because we feel powerless
to make our point. This was Gideon's dilemma.

The world is full of people who exploit and take advantage of those who are easily intimidated. Masters seek
slaves to dominate. Macho men with extra large egos seek
weak women with poor self-images to dominate in marriage. Women's libbers find mousey husbands to prove
they are the superior sex. Satan stalks the cities watching
for frightened runaways to draw them into sin. Selfish
parents vicariously seek to live their lives through their
children. Power hungry employers enjoy flinging their
power and authority around. Ministers may use the Word
of God as a lasso to rope their congregation into following
them.

Jesus said,

> *'No longer do I call you servants, for a servant does
> not know what his master is doing; but I have called
> you friends, for all things that I heard from My Father
> I have made known to you.'*[1]

Jesus does not treat His Church as His Slave, but rather
raises us **up** unto heavenly places. We are His friends
whom He loves, and the nature of His love is to **uplift us,
to release us into our full potential**. Love gives joy for

mourning, beauty for ashes, heaven for hell, grace for law, forgiveness for sin. Intimidation gives demands, threats, control and bondage.

Jesus wants us to win, but not through intimidation, rather through **Him**. He said in Matthew 16:18,

> '... *I will build my church; and the gates of hell* **shall not prevail against it**.'

Other translations read, '... *and the powers of death* **shall not subdue it**';[2] '... *and the forces of death* **shall never overpower it**';[3] '... *and the doors of Sheol* **shall not shut in on it**';[4] '... *and the powers of the underworld* **shall never overthrow it**';[5] '... *and the gates of Hades will not* **prove stronger than it**.'[6]

Here is a promise of victory, of success in the face of hell itself. The Ben Campbell Johnson Paraphrase says,

> '*I will build a community of persons who are related to* **Me**. *The* **combined forces of evil will not prevail over this community**.'

The gates of hell are erected to intimidate us into succumbing to evil. But when we know what Christ has done, not even the combined forces of evil can cause us to run in fear. People who live under the dominion of someone else do not know this truth or do not believe it.

When Jesus said this to the disciples, the Jewish people were living under the control of a well established pharisaical religion. The Pharisees and Sadducees had the entire nation spiritually intimidated because of their political corruption, religious education, clothes, their command of scriptures and position as priests. These cold-hearted priests used religious blackmail to suppress the masses.

This is why Jesus so vehemently attacked these hypo-critical priests. He exposed their motives, refused to play their tune and spoke the truth. And that is the key to freedom – knowing the truth.

Why can Jesus give us such a promise of triumph regardless of the opposition against us? Because of **who He is!** Just prior to giving this promise Jesus asked His disciples the all important question: *'Who do you say that I am?'*[7] Here is a question every single person must answer, and depending on each individual's conclusion it will mean either eternal life or eternal damnation, reign-ing with Christ or ultimate defeat. Now the disciples had come to their moment of truth. All of heaven, all of hell, and Jesus Himself were awaiting their reply. And the words that came from Peter's lips forever changed his destiny and that of multitudes since. The answer was, *'You are the Christ, the Son of the living God.'*[8]

Answering this question is the beginning of freedom for the 'intimidatee', because as long as you do not know **who Christ is and what He has done**, you will remain in angry defeat.

This was the revelation which crystallized the disciples' understanding of Jesus. He was indeed more than just a man – He was also **God!** They now realised that this man standing before them was the Creator of heaven and earth, the same One Isaiah had seen *'...sitting on the throne, high and lifted up, and the train of His robe filled the temple.'*[9] He was the One David sang to, the prophets wrote about and Adam walked with in the garden. And now He was Immanuel, God with them, in their midst. He was in this world, but not of this world. He was walking in their shoes, but not bowing to the intimidation of the religious system. Why? Because He *IS* God, He *IS* Lord, He *IS* Love, He *IS* Conqueror, He *IS* Power and **He IS the head and life of the Church!** Colossians 1:18 in the Twentieth Century New Testament says Jesus '*. . . is to the church the Source of its life.*' Ephesians 1:22–23 gives us an even clearer picture by stating that

> '*God has placed **everything** under the power of Christ and has set Him up as head of everything **for the Church**. For the Church is **His Body** and **in that Body lives fully** the One who fills the whole wide universe.*'
>
> (J.B. Phillips Translation)

In other words, Jesus was saying to His disciples that the day was coming when He would live inside of His people, the Church, by the Holy Spirit. And if they would **believe Him** and **recognise who He is**, they would **never be overthrown. Christ in them** would **build His** Church, and the gates of hell **would not prevail**. Jesus who overcame intimidation is now the One living in us!

The reason why so many fall prey to intimidators is that fear grips their minds and hearts. They cannot answer because their mind is frozen, their courage is besieged with panic. All understanding of Christ in them is gone. The fact that they are a new creation set free from the old life has not yet been realised. People who are easily intimidated fall prey to pressure because they are protecting their self-life. This we will discover in the next chapter.

## Footnotes

1. John 15:15 (NKJV)
2. Goodspeed

3.  New English Bible
4.  Lamsa
5.  Williams
6.  New International Footnote
7.  Matthew 16:15 (NKJV)
8.  Matthew 16:16 (NKJV)
9.  Isaiah 6:1 (NKJV)

# *Chapter 4*

## **The Unwanted Truth**

When we are intimidated like Moses and Gideon, we often compromise, hoping to hold on to some of our dignity, our self-life, never realising that our self-life is the very thing Jesus instructs us to lose:

> *'He who finds his life* (his self-life) *will lose it, and he who loses his life* (self-life) *for My sake will find it.'*[1]

Intimidatees are clinging, holding on to whatever they can, attempting to gain something by submitting, never realising that they **have been crucified**. What matters is not that their intimidator has allowed them to keep something dear to them but that truth prevails and evil is defeated. Moses wanted to keep the peace, Gideon did not want any problems with his fellow Israelites. He felt he already had enough with the Midianites.

This dynamic can be seen in the life of Saul. He was instructed by the prophet Samuel to *'Attack Amalek, and utterly destroy all that they have, and do not spare them.'*[2] Then in verse 9 we read,

> *'**But** Saul and the people spared fatlings, the lambs,*
> *and all that was good, and were **unwilling** to **utterly***
> ***destroy them**. But everything despised and worthless,*
> *that they utterly destroyed.'*[3]

What was Saul's reason for disobeying God? Verse 24
of 1 Samuel 15 tells us:

> *'Then Saul said to Samuel, I have sinned, for I have*
> *transgressed the **commandment** of the Lord and **your***
> ***words**, because I **feared** the people and obeyed **their***
> ***voice**.'*

Why did Saul acquiesce to the pressure of the people?
Because he **believed he would lose something** he wanted to
retain – position, wealth, power and image.

When Saul chose to obey man's word rather than God's
Word he started building on popularity, public opinion,
and pressures of special interest groups. Because of this,
God tore the Kingdom of Israel from Saul and gave it to
another, David. How ironic that the very means Saul used
to keep his kingdom (disobeying God) was the very cause
of his downfall. This is the Devil's tactic, to move us out
of faith in Christ and on to our own sufficiency. We think
we can retain our world by our own means. But Saul's
idea of how to build an empire proved fatal. And it
happened because he never realised that God's Kingdom
must be built upon God's Word – Jesus Christ. Christ
alone is the Rock upon which God's Kingdom is established. Fear and intimidation are disguised to push us into
compromise. We forget that all we have has been given to
us by God and can only be maintained by God. James
Elliott wrote,

> 'He is no fool to lose that which he cannot keep to gain that which he cannot lose.'

Throughout history people have moved forward until the Devil devised some challenge. Too often the response is **compromise**. 'We will agree to your terms if you let us keep what is precious to us.' This is nothing short of making a pact with the Devil. In this way whole nations have fallen under the fear of evil spirits. Intimidated people develop elaborate behaviours to appease the angry intimidator.

We must ask ourselves what Samuel asked Saul: Why do we give in to intimidation? What are we trying to preserve? Are we truly victorious, or are we preserving our self-life through our actions?

The intimidator is wrong because he is out to control, but the intimidatee is also wrong because he compromises the truth in order to save self.

Saul was intimidated by the people so he compromised, thinking he could retain his position. That is preserving **self** which was **crucified with Christ**. Jesus did not come to set us free from fear and intimidation so we could be proved right. He set us free so truth would prevail. But as long as the intimidatee feels victimised, he will never have to admit he is wrong. And this image is reinforced by other people who lavish pity on him. A show of sympathy only strengthens self. Samuel gave Saul no sympathy – he rebuked him for his disobedience to God. Being intimidated does not mean we are not responsible for our actions. All are commanded to live by faith in Christ, regardless of the circumstances.

Saul cowered under intimidation not because he was a victim, but because he tried to save himself. He gave in for personal gain. The intimidator wants control. The intimidatee wants to preserve self. This is the lie of the Devil. He tells the intimidatee that the only way to survive is to compromise and let the other person have his way, keeping the peace by compromising the truth.

Every minister must know this. Every Christian must realise this, or his ministry and life will be shaken to rubble. The gates of hell will always prevail over self-effort. It is only as Christ builds **His** Kingdom through His people that our victory is assured.

This truth needs to be faced if true freedom is to be experienced. Being liberated from the circumstances is not the answer. Unless the issue is dealt with in the heart, we can be certain that another situation will arise with the same results. The only answer is to be dead to self and alive to Christ.

Satan, with all his principalities, powers, might and dominion, could not prevail against Jesus in His earthly walk or in the grave. Jesus succeeded in completing His earthly mission, for in one master stroke of God's divine resurrection power, Christ was raised from the dead to reign supreme at the Father's right hand. Jesus defeated Satan because he did not attempt to save Himself. Instead He placed His life in the Father's hands.

Facing your intimidator may place you at risk so that you lose something of value. But it is right to face intimidation. In order to do this you must put self on the firing line. You must choose between losing your self-life or keeping it. Satan could not defeat Jesus and he cannot defeat us if we live as Jesus did. He is in us with the same resurrection power. *'You are of God, little children, and have overcome them'* (**Why?**) *'because **He who is in you is greater** than he who is in the world.'*[4] Again, 1 John 5:4 says,

> *'For whatsoever is born of God **overcometh the world**: and this is the victory that overcometh the world, even our faith.'*

Our faith in what? Our faith **in who Jesus Christ is in us!** Had Saul known that God's Kingdom could only be built upon Jesus Christ, the Word, he would have **succeeded**.

The question is, why did Saul acquiesce to intimidation? It was because he believed he could win in some way, only his way was through self-effort. We placate the intimidator to achieve **our** own purpose in some way. The intimidatee is often pitied, but he is living in the flesh just as much as the intimidator. It is just more subversive. Too often we judge between right and wrong by external evidences, but God looks at the heart. Appearing to be a victim can very often be an excuse to escape from repentance.

Like Saul, when the apparent victim is confronted with the truth that he is protecting himself and needs to change, he then feels worthless, as though everybody is against him. As long as the focus is on the intimidator, the victim is comfortable. But the instant the light is on the victim, he responds with horror that his innocence should be questioned.

At this point it is easier to believe the lie than the truth. The lie is, 'I am a victim.' This lie is our escape from the cross, from denying self. Intimidatees often develop relationships with intimidators so that they have a socially acceptable reason for avoiding themselves. Everybody generally focuses on the 'bad guy'. This is a cover-up to avoid Christ's command to deny self. Saul conveniently used the people as his decoy, Moses used his wife and Gideon used the Midianites. It is not always the intimidator who seeks out the weak. Both types of individuals are capable of using each other.

There is only one way to win, and Paul discovered it when he wrote,

> *'I have been crucified with Christ; it is no longer I who live, but **Christ lives in me**.'*[5]

Paul successfuly pioneered the first century Church under mountainous opposition and intimidation from the Romans because he knew that it was Christ in him (the Living Word) who was building **His** Church. Paul also wrote,

> *'When you received the person of Christ you were joined to the same fullness! Therefore, your own spiritual make-up is now full, you are complete in Christ, the fountain from which all authority and power proceeds...'*[6]

Paul experienced God's life within him and he was motivated by Him. He never suffered from spiritual fatigue, because his spirit-man was full of life. Christ was Paul's living power plant, emanating divine energy.

Paul could have easily felt intimidated, victimised by God, the world and the Devil, but he did not because he knew what it was to be dead to his self-life. Paul writes,

> *'I know how to be abased, and I know how to abound. Everywhere and in all things I have learned both to be full and to be hungry, both to abound and to suffer need. I can do all things through Christ who strengthens me.'*[7]

Paul was independent of outside events. He was free. He did not allow the world around him to dominate his decisions or actions. He responded to what Christ within him was saying and not to what his flesh, the world or the Devil were saying. Paul chose to speak when others said not to speak. He spoke out because he put Christ first and his self-life last. Paul put his self-life at risk because he knew that he had already died in Christ. It was not theology to him. It was practical reality in a real world. As long as we seek to protect our self-life, we will compromise and choose to believe the lie.

## Footnotes

1. Luke 9:24 (NKJV)
2. 1 Samuel 15:3 (NKJV)
3. 1 Samuel 15:9 (NKJV)
4. 1 John 4:4 (NKJV)
5. Galatians 2:20 (NKJV)
6. Colossians 2:9–10 (Lovett)
7. Philippians 4:12–13 (NKJV)

# Chapter 5

## Satan's Tactics

Satan attempts to deceive and thwart us by making everything look unattainable. Though the power plant is in us
the barriers are around us, just as the clouds are in front
of the sun. The Devil sends the Goliaths who roar out
their threats. Yet in these circumstances, like the
believers of yesterday, we need to be able to hear Christ
within us shout, *'The gates of hell **shall not prevail against
you**.'*

Has not the enemy attempted to eliminate the Church
in Russia through propaganda, fear, military force and
the secret police? Despite all of Satan's efforts there are
more born-again Christians in Russia today than there are
in the United States. During the Dark Ages Satan thought
he had suffocated the Church by locking the Bible behind
the closed doors of monasteries. But again, in the midst of
Europe's darkest moment, light sprang up through men
like Martin Luther. God brought reformation out of spiritual deprivation.

Satan intimidates us so that we will believe his lies.
Nations will intimidate other nations into surrendering
just by a show of force, and if they are successful they can
conquer without a single shot being fired. During World

War II Germany swallowed up several nations simply through threats and fear tactics. And those nations surrendered because they believed the lies and felt they could preserve themselves through compromise. They allowed Germany to annex their territory without giving up their lives. They did not put their trust in God to save them or their nation.

That is why surrendering to the intimidator is surrendering to the lie. John 8:44 says,

> *'When he* (the devil) *speaks a lie, he speaks of his own; for he is a liar, and the father of it.'*

As Paul said, we do not want to be ignorant of Satan's devices, and one of his devices is lying. This was why God dealt so harshly with Saul. Saul thought he was a victim of the people's intimidation, but he was really believing a lie of the Devil. Keeping the peace was the lie Moses settled for, and for Gideon it was believing he was helpless.

None of us likes to think we are believing a lie. It is more face-saving to believe we are a victim. This is the smooth, plausible story of Satan. He disguises intimidation so that we feel we have no option but to give in. In this way Satan moves us into unbelief. We forget that being in Christ always provides an answer, a miracle, a way to win.

Just as the people attempted to convince Saul to move his faith off God's Word, society today continues to pressure the Church to think that we are out of touch, old fashioned, narrow-minded and bigoted for not accepting the world's moral standards. One brazen example of this is playing with terminology, such as changing what the

Church would call abortion or murder to the more palatable word of 'contragestive'.

The French inventor of the abortion pill, Etienne-Emile Baulieu, wants to eliminate the word 'abortion' and replace it with 'contragestive'. Baulieu told *Vanity Fair* magazine,

> 'Because of the right-to-life people, abortion means a little baby that one pulls out of a mother. That is horrible. We must get rid of that word abortion.'

This is Satan's insidious attempt to sway the masses by using a safe glossary of inoffensive terms, which makes us, the Church, look bad when we call it sin.

What we call adultery or fornication, they call safe sex. What we call homosexuality, they call alternative lifestyle. These are verbal messages designed to brow-beat us into submission so that the conscience no longer convicts. Why does the Church yield to these intimidation tactics? Because of our strong faith in Christ? **NO!** Because of our love for the truth? **NO!** Because we want God to be glorified? **NO!** Because, like most intimidatees, we want to remain as comfortable as possible, preserve the peace and avoid a fight.

Saul did not stand up for Christ before the people. He was afraid for his **self**. He was not thinking of God's glory. These are the issues we must face, either as an intimidator or as an intimidatee.

The wife who continually remains silent about the husband who beats her is operating in fear, not faith in Christ. The husband who will not be the godly head of his house because of a domineering wife is weakened by fear, not faith in God's Word.

I am not talking about children who are victims of war, society or raging families, but adults who are in Christ and have the answer in their hearts. Faith in Christ will bring **freedom**. And the way to freedom is repentance and faith.

## *Chapter 6*

## Facing Our Intimidator

There comes a time when God calls the intimidatee to face the intimidator. This is an unpleasant task that Moses, Gideon and Saul all had to confront. And this is when you find out how much you have been protecting self.

There was a time in the history of Israel when it looked as though the gates of hell were prevailing. A giant, militant man named Goliath challenged any soldier of Saul's army to hand-to-hand combat. The winner of this contest was to determine which army would be the victor.

For forty days Goliath appeared before Saul's army shouting out his challenge, but so ominous and fierce was his voice and appearance that not one soldier among the entire Israelite army was willing to fight him. He was a master at frightening people with his mocking speech and guise of boldness.

This is the Devil's tactic of intimidation. Through his con-men, he immobilizes God's people. His strategy then was to use a man called Goliath. Just one look at him was so convincing that a whole army shrunk back helpless against such a formidable opponent. The effect was like that of a smooth-talking salesman whose rhetoric and aggressive personality make you feel like less-than-a-worm if you don't buy his product.

But God's Word says,

> *'For the eyes of the Lord run to and fro throughout the whole earth,* **to show himself strong on behalf of those whose heart is loyal to him.***'*[1]

God wanted to **show himself strong** on behalf of Israel, and He wants to show His power to you too. However, He needs someone who **believes in Him** more than in the roaring Goliath. He is looking for men and women of faith, who are willing to go face-to-face with their Goliaths head-on in the power of faith, despite frightening appearances.

The same tactic of intimidation was used hundreds of years earlier when Israel was living in Egypt. Exodus 1:9–12 says,

> *'And he said to his people, "Look the people of the children of Israel are* **more** *and* **mightier** *than we; come let us deal* **wisely** *with them, lest they multiply, and it happen, in the event of war, that they also join our enemies and fight against us, and so go up out of the land." Therefore they set taskmasters over them to afflict them with their burdens. And they built for Pharaoh supply cities, Pithom and Raamses. But the more they afflicted them, the* **more they multiplied** *and grew. And they were in* **dread of the children of Israel.***'*
> (NKJV)

Even though the children of Israel were greater in number, mightier in strength and frightening to the Egyptians, nonetheless it was **they** who became the slaves. This happened through intimidation. The Egyptians successfully bullied the Israelites into thinking that **they** were the weaker, inferior race and that the Egyptians were the strongest when in reality the opposite was true. That is exactly what Goliath did. He made every soldier feel inferior to him.

In the early days of my ministry there was a person who disliked me at first sight. So insistent was this person's attitude towards me that she invited a speaker to come and minister at a church where she knew I would be involved. She had set the stage by sharing her negative opinions with him in hopes that her influence could be exerted over me through him, which is exactly what happened. At the end of the service he walked right towards me and prophesied. By the end of the prophecy I was depressed, discouraged and bewildered.

It was not until the following morning when the Holy Spirit revealed to me the truth of the matter that my joy returned. The spirit of manipulation, oppression and intimidation was broken as my eyes were re-focused on God's truth and away from her words. A strength stirred in my spirit that enabled me to rise up and face those curses and declare them **untrue**.

God raised up Moses to break the spirit of fear over Israel, but to do it he had to **face** his wife and the enemy – Pharaoh. In Saul's case it was going to require the same action: somebody would have to stand up to Goliath face-to-face.

Satan has immobilized Christians, churches and moves of the Spirit of revival through these Goliath-like tactics of intimidation. Saul's entire army had come to a standstill because of one man. How often whole moves of God are cut short because of one obstacle. Denominations become derailed due to criticism, and Christian ministries fall prey to ineptness as disapproval is expressed. God is looking for Christians who will run **forward**, not flee. Goliath was like hell's gates, parading defiantly before Israel, and the only way to demolish him was for David to face him and aggressively press past him. This was the only way the gates of hell could **not** prevail against Israel.

Satan's gates are erected to stop the advancing Church, and those gates will prevail if we, like Saul's army, remain silent and stationary. But, if we go forward as David did, those gates will collapse. There is no need for gates if no-one desires to move. Jesus said, '*I will **build**.*' 'Build' is an action word describing forward movement.

In facing our Goliaths we will have to change by believing our **self-life** is crucified because it is not worth preserving. Christ has resurrected a new you, one who lives **for** Christ, **because** of Christ and **by** Christ.

How do we face our Goliaths? How do we break the control and fear we feel? First, we must speak the truth in love, determined to confront our intimidator head on, whether he is going to love us or hate us. Secondly, we must not flinch or cower even if our body, emotions and thoughts experience negative reactions; shaking limbs, trembling voice, feelings of fear and worthlessness, confusion about what the real issue is, and an inability to articulate the problem clearly. These are all natural reactions of our humanity, and we are to regard all these responses as unimportant. Do not allow them to stop you from doing what you need to do. Act out of your heart, your spirit, where the Holy Spirit lives to strengthen you.

It may seem as though you are in two worlds; the physical sensation of fear on the one side, and your spirit alive with faith and courage on the other. Follow your heart. Intimidatees remain trapped as long as they live by their feelings and thoughts. Freedom begins when you act upon the **truth**, regardless of how you feel. Moses and Gideon did not suddenly feel different, they simply saw the truth and **acted upon it**.

## Living in Blame or Blessing

When a person experiences abuse and overpowering circumstances, self-pity seems justifiable. The man who waited at the pool of Bethesda to be healed of his crippling disease attempted to step into the water when it was moving, but everybody else jumped in before him and preempted his healing. For thirty eight years he watched others walk away from this mysterious pool healed while he remained crippled.

Who would blame him for feeling sorry for himself, for lashing out at the injustice life had dealt him? As the years went on this pool became more of a curse than a blessing. He had personally witnessed the insensitivity and cruelty of man. No-one had helped him. When the waters were stirred and the opportunity for healing came, nobody thought of anybody else but themselves.

When Jesus saw him He asked, *'Do you want to be made well?'*[2] What an odd question to ask someone who had lived by this pool for thirty eight years hoping against hope for the slightest chance of health. From all outward appearances he did want healing, but Jesus always exposes our hearts, our motive. The crippled man's answer is revealing:

> *'Sir, I have no man to put me into the pool when the water is stirred up; but while I am coming, another steps down before me.'*[3]

Instead of answering Jesus with a straight 'Yes', his true colours come out by blaming other people for his misfortune. This is victim mentality.

Today children blame parents for their behaviour, parents blame schools for not doing their job. Husbands blame wives and wives their husbands. People in debt blame the economy, the rich accuse the poor and the poor the rich. Criminals point the finger at society and society blames governments. All see themselves as victims. Many Christians blame the Devil and God in the same breath for their mishaps.

There is a victim psychology that says you are not responsible for your sin, which is what Saul was attempting to use. But God teaches differently: '...*all have sinned and fall short of the glory of God.*'[4] All are responsible for how they feel, think and behave. We cannot always control life, but we can **choose** how we respond to it, and that is the difference between the victim and the victor.

There are true victims – children who are abused by parents, relatives killed by a drunken driver, people conned out of their life savings. Yet even these people are still responsible to forgive, love their enemy, bless those who curse them.

Life touches all of us and we can respond either as a victim or as a victor. The victim says, 'I am hurt.' The victor says,

> '*Surely He has borne our griefs and carried our sorrows ... But He was wounded for our transgressions, He was bruised for our iniquities; the chastisement for our peace was upon Him. And by **His stripes we are healed**.*'[5]

The victim says, 'I am not responsible for my actions. Do

you know what my mother, my brother, my uncle did to me?' The victor says,

> *'Therefore, if anyone is in Christ, he is a new creation; old things have passed away; behold, all things have become **new**.'*[6]

The victim feels anger, resentment and bitter envy towards others who are happy. And if others do not agree with their assessment, then they fall into depression. The victor however, has love for their enemies, blesses those who curse, wants good for those who hate them and prays for those who spitefully use them.[7] Victims live in suspicion, trusting nobody for fear that they will be mistreated again. Victors believe,

> *'God has not given us* (them) *a spirit of fear, but of power and of love and of a sound mind.'*[8]

The crippled man went from being victim to victor by believing the words of Jesus, and he became **whole**.[9]

Jesus was the ultimate victim of **our sin**. He did not deserve to die, to suffer, to be separated from the Father, to be ridiculed, mocked, beaten and shamed. Nothing Jesus did ever warranted the injustice and hatred He encountered. Yet His final words to a hostile world were, *'Father, forgive them, for they do not know what they do.'*[10] Jesus demonstrated that forgiveness is the pathway from victim to victor. God raised Him up and enthroned Him at His right hand to reign forever in love, not to blame mankind for His misery while on earth.

Saul and his army remained paralysed while David acted upon God's Word. For forty days the soldiers sat

around the campfire affirming each other's justifications
as to why they were legitimate victims. Victims often band
together with other victims to form an alliance that ver-
ifies their situation.

Faith says, *'I can do all things through Christ who
strengthens me.'*[11] Even though your emotions are screaming with fear, face your intimidator by the Spirit. All the
soldiers believed their fears and stood immobilized and
intimidated. David believed God's word and moved into
freedom.

In 2 Chronicles 32:1, 9, 16–17 we have the account of
intimidation. The King of Assyria came against Judah
with his mighty army. He laid seige against Jerusalem and
the surrounding cities. This was an attempt to win through
intimidation. The captain of the Assyrian army rode over
to Jerusalem, stood outside the city wall and read a letter
to King Hezekiah and the Jews within the city. This is
what he read:

> *'Now do not let Hezekiah deceive you and mislead
> you like this. Do not believe him, for no god of any
> nation or kingdom has been able to deliver his people
> from my hand or the hand of my fathers. How much
> less will your god deliver you from my hand!'*

(NIV)

Not only did the captain do this day by day, but he also
sent letters to Hezekiah's employees saying,

> *'Sennacherib's officers spoke further against the Lord
> and against his servant Hezekiah. The king also wrote
> letters insulting the Lord, the God of Israel, and say-
> ing this against him: "Just as the gods of the peoples of*

*the other lands did not rescue their people from my hand, so the god of Hezekiah will not rescue his people from my hand."'* (NIV)

Satan came as a roaring lion, confident, daring, impudent and audacious. He was out to convince the Jews that he was right and God was wrong. Satan knows that if we will believe the lie, he can hold us in bondage. If we believe we have no choice, we will give up.

In this case Satan came as a roaring lion out to devour. With all the boldness and confidence he had, he proclaimed a lie. And his lie was, 'Your God cannot save you. You may as well become my slave and make the best of it.' This has been the philosophy of all dictators throughout history. They believe that if they tell a big enough lie long enough, and forcefully enough, the common people will believe them.

Satan has not changed. Today he dresses up his lies with media presentations, computer graphics, marketing techniques, colour saturation and dolby sound. Now it is the professionals, scientists, experts, strategists and image makers who speak lies with authority. Their words are smooth, their logic confusing and their smile convincing. They seem so plausible that many give up their faith in God's Word and buckle under the **intimidating** methods of Satan. This is why Peter said '*...resist him steadfast in the faith.*' We need to **resist** and *'fight the good fight of faith.'*

Hezekiah served as a good example. He did not fall for Satan's intimidating smokescreen tactics but **prayed and cried unto heaven**. He did not give way to fear but picked up his faith and said, '**No!** My God **will** save me.' God responded to his faith and that night:

'...*the Lord sent an angel, who annihilated all the
fighting men and the leaders and officers in the camp
of the Assyrian king. So he withdrew to his own land
in disgrace. And when he went into the temple of his
god, some of his sons cut him down with the sword.*'[12]

God is **touched** by our **infirmities** and **moved** by our
**faith**. His love has no bounds for those who put their trust
in Him. For He '*spoiled principalities and powers, He*
(Jesus) *made a show of them openly, triumphing over
them in it.*' Fear and intimidation lead to defeat and
compromise. Faith leads to victory!

Can't you hear the Devil using the same tactics on
Moses when he said, 'Who made you a ruler and a judge
over us?' How the Devil must have goaded and accused
Moses with that lie while he lived in the desert. Day and
night he was out to intimidate Moses with fear: 'You
failed! You are a murderer, a worthless shepherd.' Moses
probably believed these lies from time to time. But he did
not give up. Though he ran, though he failed, he still
prayed and cried out to God like Hezekiah, and God
came to his rescue. God put Satan in his place and called
his bluff. Moses the unknown shepherd went down into
Egypt with faith and power in his heart saying to Pharaoh,
'Let my people go!' Moses made the Word of God come
to pass not only freeing three million of God's people but
utterly destroying Egypt, Satan's stronghold! **This is the
kind of God we serve.**

For those forty years in the desert Moses experienced a
constant barrage of **false accusations** sent to **intimidate**
and **pressure** him. Satan tried to **embarrass** Moses for
believing God's Word. How subtle this is. You are with a
group of people and Jesus is mentioned but you are too
embarrassed to speak up. Why? Intimidation.

There comes a time when we must **turn the tide** and accept God's Word for our lives. As Jude said,

> '... *contend earnestly for the faith which was once for all delivered to the saints.*'[13]

The Gospel is still true, it has never changed and it **will**, **will**, **will** work for us today just as it did for Hezekiah. We cannot allow ourselves to think that God will not deliver us. We must not believe the lie that Jesus is unreachable and unconcerned about us. Jesus not only showed but proved His willingness to save, heal and deliver on the cross. David believed and therefore said,

> '*Yea, though I walk through the valley of the shadow of death, I will fear no evil; for You are with me, Your rod and Your staff, they comfort me.*'[14]

This is the kind of heart and faith God found in David. His faith had already faced a lion and a bear, sustained him and his flock in the heat and the cold, and formed a living relationship with the Almighty. Yes, David knew faith could move any mountain, part any sea, heal any sickness and deliver any family out of any tragedy, as long as he was willing to put it into action and go forward.

## Footnotes

1. 2 Chronicles 16:9 (NKJV)
2. John 5:6 (NKJV)
3. John 5:7 (NKJV)
4. Romans 3:23 (NKJV)
5. Isaiah 53:4–5 (NKJV)
6. 2 Corinthians 5:17 (NKJV)
7. Matthew 5:44 (NKJV)
8. 2 Timothy 1:7 (NKJV)

9.   John 5:8 (NKJV)
10.  Luke 23:34 (NKJV)
11.  Philippians 4:13 (NKJV)
12.  2 Chronicles 32:21 (NIV)
13.  Jude 3 (NKJV)
14.  Psalm 23:4 (NKJV)

# *Chapter 7*

## How David Faced Goliath

Listen to David's confession of faith as he was challenged by this Goliath:

> *'For who is this uncircumcised Philistine that he should defy the armies of the living God?'*[1]

David was not intimidated, but rather he was filled with righteous indignation that this agent of the Devil should defy the armies of the living God. This needs to be our attitude toward the Goliaths we are facing. Whether they threaten us in the form of a spiritual impasse, sickness, loneliness, breakdown in relationships or financial pressure, we need to shout, 'What is this sickness that it should defy the temple of the Holy Spirit?'

No matter how fierce, frightening or persistent our enemy is, Christ within us has promised that, *'the gates of hell shall not prevail against us!'* God expects us to face life head on, to **overcome** Goliaths with the knowledge that we have **already won through Christ before the battle begins!**

Paul echoed this same note of triumph when he wrote,

'Now thanks be to God, which **always causeth us to triumph in Christ**.'[2]

Let **His** name be praised! **God always, always,** causes us to win! We are destined to overcome. In Christ we were created to succeed. We are not the losers, the down and out, the tailend, the discouraged. We **are** the head, raised and seated with Christ, **as more than conquerors!**

This is why David could tackle his Goliath, because he had concluded that Goliath was already a defeated foe. David never flinched, never hesitated, but simply advanced forward with his trust in God's victory. This is how faith works. It marches forward with irresistible progress because it sees with Christ's reigning eye the enemy's demise.

When this truth becomes revelation to you it means the Devil has lost himself another customer – you. It means your life is not spent protecting self but projecting **Christ**.

The fact that our Goliaths have already been defeated needs to be forever settled in our hearts. Paul said,

'On the cross He (Jesus) **stripped** the demonic powers and authorities of their power, and made a public spectacle of them, as if they had been captives in a victor's triumphal procession.'[3]

John tells us,

'For this purpose the Son of God was manifested, that he might destroy the works of the devil.'[4]

That word destroy also means, 'break, defeat, render inoperative, paralyse, put out of commission and dethrone the Devil.'

We do not have to hope, as I'm sure that many of Saul's army did, that our Goliath will stumble and break his neck as he walks into the valley. We have to face life and people.

You may be saying to yourself, 'Dealing with a one-time Goliath who is an outsider is much easier to face than the person I have to live with day in and day out. I cannot just come against him in the name of the Lord and then it is all over.'

Admittedly interpersonal relationships are much harder to deal with, but the answer is still the same. David won over Goliath, but he also won in his relationship to King Saul. David could not face Saul once and then it was over, he had to face him daily. For many years Saul sought to intimidate David, to pressure him into compromising his faith in God.

David had to hide, run and fight. David was hunted, slandered, hated, falsely accused and treated unjustly. Yet he did not compromise and become one of Saul's 'yes men'. David did not take matters into his own hands, rise up in rebellion and revenge. He learned to trust God, daily take up his cross and praise God in the face of injustice. David did not develop a victim mentality, he daily forgave, he daily denied self, he daily put his trust in God.

## What Are We Avoiding?

Nehemiah was a man whose heart God had touched with a desire to see a nation restored. But in order to fulfil his call he was first going to have to face the king first. God's call put him in direct conflict with his own self-life; he would have to lay it down and risk it in order to obey Christ.

Nehemiah was the wine taster whose job was to test the wine for the king of Babylon to discover any poisons. His job description also consisted of appearing joyful in the king's presence. Yet now he was sad because of Jerusalem's desolation. The only way he could help was by asking the king's permission to leave work as well as request written authority to rebuild Jerusalem's walls.

Was he afraid? Yes! Was he intimidated? Yes! Was his life at risk for appearing sad before the king at an inappropriate time? Yes! But Nehemiah faced the king and the consequences anyway. He put his life in God's hands. He did not choose to save his life by remaining silent. He denied his life by speaking up.

There is no other way. Just like Nehemiah, we must be willing to lay our lives down, to do whatever needs to be done and to face all obstacles for God's will. Avoiding the issue is pleasing self, pampering self, throwing our cross down and living in fear.

Esther had to face another king before salvation could come to the Jewish people. Daniel also had to face the law before God's name would be glorified. The apostles had to face Jesus after they all deserted Him in the garden before Pentecost could come. Without exception, as soon as we choose to walk in the spirit we will face the flesh. If one person in a relationship begins living in the spirit, conflict arises. Spirit is spirit and flesh is flesh. They are like oil and water. Whether like David we have to face a Goliath once or a Saul day after day, it still needs to be done.

Paul said that the

> '*carnal mind is enmity against God: for it is not subject to the law of God nor **indeed** can be. So then, they that are in the flesh cannot please God.*'[5]

There can be no mixture. It is all or nothing.

Most of us would like the other person to change first, or for the obstacles in our relationships to be removed. That will not happen until we reach heaven. And the truth of the matter is the king was not Nehemiah's problem, nor was the law Daniel's. The king was not Esther's problem, nor was Jesus for the disciples or Saul for David. They themselves, their own self-life, was the real obstacle. Our husbands, wives, friends, local church, students or workers are not our problem. It is us. The only question is, will we do what is right and face ourselves? Zipporah was not Moses' problem, the Midianites were not Gideon's problem, it was the unbelief in their own hearts that was the real issue.

We cannot hope our bills away. We cannot simply ignore our problems. We cannot expect Satan to take pity on us or to feel sympathetic towards our cries. He has a fixed nature of evil and destruction. He only knows one limit and that is the shed blood and finished work of Christ's atonement. As Moses faced Pharaoh, David his Goliath and Jesus the cross, so we too must be willing to face our Goliaths. And we can if we know that our victory, our protection, our joy, our life is in our identification with Christ's accomplished work of redemption. Why is this? Because when Christ died, **we** died; when Christ rose from the grave, **we** rose **with** Him; when He was glorified, **we** sat down **with** Him at the Father's right hand.

What is the result of dying **with** Christ? Like Christ we too are now **dead** to sin, to the flesh, to the spirit of this world. In other words, we can be non-responsive to their influence. David was not intimidated by Goliath's threats. He considered himself dead to Goliath and therefore could not be touched by him.

Another translation of Romans 6:11 says,

> *'Let us consider ourselves as actually dead to sin.'*

Ask yourself this question: How would a dead person respond to temptation, threats, pressures and lies? He would not. You can yell, intimidate, slap, throw dirt in the air, jump up and down shouting at the corpse and what will it do? **Nothing! It is dead!** That is exactly how **we** are to be in regard to sin and the Devil's lies.

I can just see Goliath becoming more and more unnerved as none of his tactics worked on David. Why should David fear? How could Goliath kill someone who was already dead?

Christians through the centuries have been willing to face death because as far as they were concerned, they had already died in Christ. This is not theological jargon, it must become a living truth worked out and lived out in our everyday lives. The apostle Paul faced death time and time again, but for him the fear of death had been left in the grave. He lived in resurrection life, a life so powerful that none could kill him until Christ decided it was time for him to go home.

This is the result of **our** resurrection **with** Christ, that just as Christ came out of the grave a victor and conqueror, so we came out of the spiritual grave victors and conquerors. Paul writes,

> *'...**Just as** Christ was raised from the dead by the glory of the Father, **even so we also should walk in newness of life**. For if **we** have been **united together** in the likeness of His death, certainly **we** also shall be in the likeness of His resurrection.'*[6]

So this is the secret, that **just as** Christ rose as a conqueror over sin, sickness, debt, fear and the Devil, **so did we!** In other words, our spirit-man is filled with the same new life that raised Christ from the dead and made Him alive. Paul excitedly writes,

> *'May you experience the incredible outburst of his power in us who rely on his might and his abundant energy. This same energy working in Christ raised him from the dead and gave him spiritual victory and authority over every ruler.'*[7]

This is how David fought Goliath: **In Christ's resurrection power**. David **knew** that since he had been raised with Christ, he too had authority over Goliath. John said,

> *'All that has received the new life from God **conquers** the world. And this is the power that has conquered the world – **our faith**.'*[8]

Again the Phillips translation says,

> *'. . . for God's heredity within us will always conquer the world outside us. In fact this faith of ours is the only way the world has been conquered.'*

Our faith in who Christ is **in us** and what He has done **for us** at Calvary is what makes us conquerors.

Let me sum up what our death and resurrection now mean to us in practical terms. Our inner man has been created, equipped and made fully capable of being sensitive, alive to and governed by God's Spirit, while at the same time dead and non-responsive to sin. This is something that happened when we were born-again, **but it is**

**activated into a life-style by faith**. Exercising faith in this truth will develop our sensitivity to Christ, which in turn will give us more ability to exercise our deadness to sin.

This is how David faced Goliath: He was practising God's presence in the wilderness while caring for his sheep. This is a daily walk developed through praying, reading the Word, meditating on God and worshipping Him.

One day in prayer the Holy Spirit spoke to me and said, 'You are not in the flesh but in the spirit.' Immediately I ran to Romans 8:9 and reread that verse a hundred times. God was stating a **fact**. Something had already taken place. '**I was in the spirit**.' In other words, my true life is **now being lived out in my spirit man, not in my flesh**. He was saying more. He now wanted me to **live like it is true, to practise it**. Giving in to fear and intimidation is not living this new life. It is living the way we used to live before we were in Christ.

David was living out his faith believing he was dead to sin and alive to God as he fought Goliath, and so must we. **We must live what we really are in Christ, not** what the flesh sees, feels or hears. What God said to me, He has said to all: 'We are **not** in the flesh, but **in** the Spirit.'

Our spirit man **is** alive to God and dead to sin, but if we are governed by the flesh we will never know this. Living in the flesh means we will be forced to fight spiritual battles with carnal weapons (Saul's armour) which results in certain defeat every time.

## Footnotes

1.    1 Samuel 17:26 (NKJV)
2.    2 Corinthians 2:14 (NKJV)
3.    Colossians 2:15 (Barclay)
4.    1 John 3:8 (NKJV)

5.    Romans 8:7–8 (NKJV)
6.    Romans 6:4–5 (NKJV)
7.    Ephesians 1:19–20 (Jordan)
8.    1 John 5:4 (20th Century C.R.)

# *Chapter 8*

## Choose Your Weapons

David could have been tempted to fight with Saul's armour. All soldiers wore armour in those days, especially when faced with an opponent like Goliath. A choice had to be made between the natural weapons or the Spirit. Paul describes this conflict between the flesh and the Spirit in Galatians 5:16–17:

> '*But I say, walk and live habitually in the Holy Spirit – responsive to and controlled and guided by the Spirit; then you will certainly not gratify the cravings and desires of the flesh – of human nature without God. For the desires of the flesh are opposed to the Holy Spirit, and the (desires of the) Spirit are opposed to the flesh (Godless human nature); for these are antagonistic to each other – continually withstanding and in conflict with each other – so that you are not free but are prevented from doing what you desire to do.*'[1]

David followed the Spirit. He put his faith in God's ways. Being united in Christ's death and resurrection means we have died to man's ways and we now live to the **way** God wants us to live. God wanted David to fight with a sling and a stone. Saul wanted David to fight with armour. But because David was **alive to Christ**, he battled God's way. As we go forward in the Spirit to face our wives, husbands, teenagers, employers, or whoever may be our intimidator, they no longer have any hold over us because we are in the Spirit and they are in the natural. As long as Moses fought with his wife Zipporah using natural weapons (keeping the peace), he remained in fear of her. The moment he moved in the Spirit and used God's weapons of obedience to His Word, Moses was free.

In the natural Goliath was a superior soldier, which meant that if David had fought him man-to-man, armour-to-armour, Goliath would have won. And in the natural realm your Goliath may also be stronger than you. This is why Satan wants us to fight with carnal weapons, because we will surely lose. But if, like David, we use God's supernatural weapons, '... *which are strong through God to the pulling down of strongholds*', we will win every time. Fighting people with arguments, unforgiveness or subversiveness will not achieve freedom. Only the truth brings authentic freedom.

## Furthermore

**Furthermore we are also seated with Christ**. Paul says of Christ and us,

> '*It is that same mighty power that raised Christ from the dead **and seated** him on the place of honour at God's right hand in Heaven, **far, far above** any other kind of ruler or dictator or leader,*' '*and lifted **us up** from the grave into glory along with Christ, where **we sit with him** in the heavenly realms – **all because of what Christ Jesus did.**'*[2]

Being alive to God in our spirit man means being aware of our authority in Christ.

David understood this and that is why he said to the soldiers,

> *'Let no man's heart fail because of him* (Goliath); *your servant will go and fight with this Philistine.'*[3]

David fought when no-one else would because he saw himself dead to Satan's lies. He knew he was an overcomer in Christ's kingdom. David acted just like Jesus because his faith had made him one with Christ. Christ facing sin at Calvary for all of us was reenacted in David as he did battle **in the place** of all the other soldiers.

And what were the results? Saul's army joined in David's victory over Goliath by storming the Philistines and plundering their land. Now we can share in Christ's victory over sin, Satan and fear by activating our faith in Christ's death, resurrection and glorification.

We need to accept the challenge by picking up our sling and stones and running towards our Goliath. The sling is our faith and the stones are the words of God. By acting upon the victory Christ has won for us through our union with Christ's death, resurrection and glorification and believing Him when He said, *'the gates of hell shall not prevail against you,'* we too can win as David did in the face of our Goliath.

**Footnotes**

1. Galatians 5:16–17 (Amplified Bible)
2. Ephesians 1:19–21, 2:6 (Living Bible)
3. 1 Samuel 17:32 (NKJV)

# PART II

# Looking at the Intimidator

## The Other Side

We have looked at people victimised by circumstances, other people or Satan. And because of this they developed a victim mentality that very often justified their compromise. Now we turn our attention to the intimidators, who they are, how they operate and God's pathway of change for them.

Shakespeare wrote so insightfully:

> 'All the world's a stage
> And all the men and women merely players:
> They have their exits and their entrances
> And one man in his time plays many parts.'
>
> (*As You Like It*, Act II, Scene 7)

The good news is that Jesus Christ can set us free from playing a role that is personally and interpersonally destructive. There is hope for people who are deeply engrained in their personality. To the Peters and Pauls, the Marthas and Sauls, God extends His patient hand of grace and power.

> '*For God is **at work in you**, both to will and to work for His good pleasure.*'          (Philippians 2:13)

# Chapter 9

## Peter – His Secret Side

Peter was a natural leader. He was strong, bold and quick with his ideas. He was the kind of person who probably intimidated others without him even being conscious of doing so. He was also a deeply spiritual man. Jesus chose him as one of His first disciples. It was Peter's boat that Jesus chose to demonstrate His miracle-power in catching the over-abundance of fish. Peter was the one with the revelation that Jesus was the Christ. Peter paid their taxes with money from the mouth of a fish. He was among the inner circle of friends closest to Jesus, and finally Peter was the one to walk on the water twice.

He must have been a difficult man with which to compete. Peter was a man's man, rough, quick-tempered, strong and sharp. There was no doubt about it. He was world leadership material. This was not the kind of person who needed his ego built up. Yet it did seem as though Jesus encouraged him through all those special privileges. Jesus chose him because he was good leadership material. He saw in Peter the potential of a world class reformer.

You might say Peter was a benevolent intimidator. Not all domineering people are evil or unwanted. As a matter of fact, many of them are in leadership positions, and highly effective both in secular and Christian work. They know how to get things done and are generally intelligent. It is these characteristics that irritate the people who feel inferior to them. It would be easier for people to feel victimized and manipulated, if intimidators were not so seemingly gifted.

People like Peter who are aggressive, sharp, movers and shakers, also have a soft side, moments when their tenderness comes shining through and everything seems bright and beautiful. Many relationships start because the individual is able to see beyond the aggressive, controlling side and touch the intimidator's caring heart. The only trick with these kinds of relationship is finding out which side of the person's personality will eventually prove itself to be the stronger of the two. All too often it is the intimidation trait that slowly overshadows and becomes dominant.

Jesus called Peter knowing this about him. The existence of sin or a personality fault does not negate our status as Christians. Jesus was able to see Peter's inner man. He knew his potential. Jesus had three years to help Peter become the right kind of leader, strong yet tender, determined yet caring.

Confronting our intimidator is not easy, and loving one is even harder. They have numerous devices for deflecting people from confronting them. And people do not confront them because they do not want to bear the brunt of their reaction. Jesus chose to do this, and over the course of the next three years, Peter was confronted on his impetuousness, his desire for position, his rash behaviour and extra large ego. But his supreme moment came as Jesus was about to be crucified.

They were in the Upper Room. It was one of the most

intimate occasions the disciples had with Jesus. And it was in this environment that Jesus turned to Peter and said,

> *'Simon, Simon! Indeed, Satan has asked for you, that he may sift you as wheat.'*[1]

Imagine Jesus saying this to you; that Satan himself was personally plotting to destroy you. I am sure all the other disciples were pleased that Peter was the target and not them. Maybe they were even happy, thinking Peter deserved it for always thinking he was so special. Most people enjoy it when an intimidator is intimidated, when they are having to take a dose of the same medicine they give out. But this was not the heart of Jesus, because in the next verse He says,

> *'But I have prayed for you, that your faith should not fail; and when you have returned to Me, strengthen your brethren.'*[2]

Peter must have been overjoyed that Jesus was personally praying for him, but why did He mention faith failing and returning, and why was Jesus discussing this openly among close friends?

By now Peter did not like the way this conversation was going. Everything Jesus was saying was contrary to his image. It was an offence to his manhood. I can just hear Peter thinking, 'I have been with You, Jesus, for three years. My business has suffered because I have not paid any attention to it. My wife feels like a widow because I am hardly ever at home any more. Why do You think I would go anywhere or fall away? And why are You making these accusations in front of all my closest friends? Don't You realise this is belittling?'

Peter, like most aggressive and strong people, did not like admitting his faults. His pride was a mighty fortress protecting him from anything that cut across his self-portrait. Peter did not like being called a quitter after all the time, money and effort he had put into following Jesus. So, in vindicating tones, Peter speaks up, *'Lord, I am ready to go with You, both to prison and to death.'*[3]

This statement was an affirmation of everything Peter saw himself to be: Mr Macho, the man who could go the distance, the man who would back down from nothing. He had proved over the past three years that he could handle the crowds, cast out demons, walk on water, bounce back from Jesus' rebukes and even take the scorn of the religious community. Why would Jesus think he would leave now?

But Jesus did not stop with that. He drove the nail home by saying,

> *'I tell you, Peter, the rooster will not crow this day before you will deny three times that you know Me.'*[4]

This was the final blow to Peter's manhood. It was against all Peter ever believed about himself. He had braved the sea on many dangerous occasions. He had faced death before, and as far as he was concerned he could face it again. Peter had spent his whole life learning how to be a 'real man'. Strong, dominant, assertive, these were the characteristics of true manliness. Jesus had hurt Peter. His very suggestion was outrageous.

But his concept of being Mr Macho was the very thing Jesus had been wanting to help Peter with. Peter's whole security came from his identity as the dominating male. It was his god, only he did not know it.

It was soon after, when Jesus was arrested, that we read, *'Peter followed at a distance.'*[5] It was beginning to happen. Peter was distancing himself from Jesus. Jesus no longer held the position of a winner. This successful charismatic miracle-worker who captivated audiences all over Israel was now a prisoner. Peter found this hard to cope with.

In one way intimidators, people who are movers and shakers, do not like being around losers. They despise them because losers are everything intimidators work so hard not to be. On the other hand intimidators need weak people because they feed on them to boost their own abilities. That is why so many strong people marry or form relationships with weaker partners. It gives them a sense of power. It all depends on whether or not there is some personal gain in keeping the relationship as to whether they remain around the other person.

Peter stayed very close to Jesus when He was popular, but his true character flaw was beginning to show. God will do this with all intimidators. He will bring them to the cross, He will expose their true heart which has been so well camouflaged by their assertiveness. This was Peter's key moment.

> *'Now when they had kindled a fire in the midst of the courtyard and sat down together, Peter sat among them. And a certain servant girl, seeing him as he sat by the fire, looked intently at him, and said, "This man was also with Him."'*[6]

Peter's moment of truth had arrived. His entire self-image, his manhood, his whole foundation for being, was challenged – and by a girl! How embarrassing, how degrading, for a woman to challenge the man of the year.

Intimidators, or dominating people, also have difficulty with the opposite sex. Some men of this nature view women as a species just below them, and women who are out to prove their libertarianism see men as objects to step on. For Peter this was the height of insult, to be uncovered by a girl, yet it was God's way of piercing Peter's male defensive armour.

Peter was true to form. He flatly denied the accusation, saying *'Woman, I do not know Him.'*[7] Intimidators are highly skilled at making other people feel stupid, and I am sure Peter's tone suggested that this girl could not have been further from the truth. Perhaps his tone was angry, or patronizing, sarcastic or degrading – all techniques used by assertive people to make their point. But God was not going to let Peter off so easily this time:

> *'And after a little while another saw him and said, "You also are of them."'*[8]

Now Peter the intimidator was being cornered. The Holy Spirit was allowing the weight of the cross, which Jesus was about to bear, to weigh heavily on Peter's shoulders. He lashed out saying, *'Man, I am not!'* The victimizer now felt like the victim. Even in this highly confrontational moment Peter did not recognise his own behaviour. His defence mechanisms were still held firmly in place. His self-life was screaming for survival. The words of Christ remained hidden:

> *'Whoever seeks to save his life will lose it, and whoever loses his life will preserve it.'*[9]

Peter was fighting for his self-life, to preserve his image.

But Jesus did not give up. His love confronted Peter once again:

> *'Then after about an hour had passed, another confidently affirmed, saying, "Surely this fellow also was with Him, for he is a Galilean." But Peter said, "Man, I do not know what you are saying." And immediately, while he was still speaking, the rooster crowed. And the **Lord turned and looked at Peter**. And Peter remembered the word of the Lord, how He had said to him, "Before the rooster crows, you will deny Me three times." Then Peter went out and wept bitterly.'*[10]

The iron man finally cracked. His life-long defences crumbled under the mighty hand of God's love, for that is what the look of Jesus was. Throughout his whole life Peter saw himself as Mr Macho, when in reality he was a coward. Unthinkable, inconceivable! The true heart of the intimidator was exposed. He hurt and bled like all other people, only he tried not to show it.

If Peter had gone on in ministry without confronting this issue, he would have built a kingdom for himself and not for Christ. Now he saw himself as he really was, a frightened human being who had been running from the truth all his life. Now Jesus brought the truth to set him **free**. The truth revealed to Peter that self was not capable of overcoming the world, that self was incapable of truly loving his fellow man, that in the end self would always look out for number one. Self and Christ were too opposing kingdoms.

Peter was now as much upon the cross as Jesus. Peter was dying on the inside. His whole life crumbled before him. He had failed. The one thing he feared the most had happened. It must have been a rare occasion for Peter to cry. It is not the thing macho men do. But those tears were of great importance. I am sure they were tears of self-pity because he had been caught, but they were also tears of repentance.

How hard it must have been for Peter to face the other disciples, but even more so to face Jesus; but he did. Peter was not all bad. It is very easy to judge intimidating people too severely. Peter came back to face the music. He had learned the greatest lesson for a man of his temperament – how to humble himself. He confessed his sin and faced the consequences. Peter was willing to lose his self-life, and because of this Peter was the one God used on the day of Pentecost to lead three thousand people to Christ. God exalted him because he was willing to humble himself even though it was the hard way.

Now Peter's temperament was under the control of the Holy Spirit. He was a new man, no longer attempting to make life happen his way but allowing Christ to build His Kingdom **His way**. In Peter's epistles we hear of a very different person who wrote,

> *'All flesh is as grass, and all the glory of man as the flower of the grass. The grass withers, and its flower falls away, but the word of the Lord endures forever.'*

> *'God resists the proud, but gives grace to the humble. Therefore humble yourselves under the mighty hand of God, that He may exalt you in due time.'*[11]

There is hope, not only for people who feel like victims, but also for the dominators!

And what is that hope? Dead to self and alive to Christ!

## Footnotes

1. Luke 22:31 (NKJV)
2. Luke 22:32 (NKJV)
3. Luke 22:33 (NKJV)
4. Luke 22:34 (NKJV)
5. Luke 22:54 (NKJV)
6. Luke 22:55–56 (NKJV)
7. Luke 22:57 (NKJV)
8. Luke 22:58 (NKJV)
9. Luke 17:33 (NKJV)
10. Luke 22:59–62 (NKJV)
11. 1 Peter 1:24–25; 5:5–6 (NKJV)

# *Chapter 10*

## Martha the Manipulator, Mary the Humble

To understand Martha and Mary's relationship we need to look at two events in their lives. The first one is in Luke 10:38–42.

> *'As Jesus and his disciples were on their way, he came to a village where a woman named Martha opened her home to him. She had a sister called Mary, who sat at the Lord's feet listening to what he said. But Martha was distracted by all the preparations that had to be made. She came to him and asked, "Lord, don't you care that my sister has left me to do the work by myself? Tell her to help me!"*
>
> *"Martha, Martha," the Lord answered, "you are worried and upset about many things, but only one thing is needed. Mary has chosen what is better, and it will not be taken away from her."'*

Imagine Martha thundering into the dining room and **yelling** at Jesus! Now that is an assertive personality. But to Martha it was perfectly natural. Mary was not helping her with the food. An honoured guest was in her home and nobody was even offering to help. Someone had to get the job done, there were responsibilities, an etiquette code to uphold and schedules to keep. And Martha was just that sort of person, directive, a natural leader.

In the working world, Martha would have been called bossy, pushy, a hard driver. She was the stereotype authoritarian who liked to take over, be in charge, tell others what to do. If she was running an organization she would be the type of boss who was heavy on authority, keeping her finger in every pie, always wanting to know everything, even to the point of control.

Jesus did not, however, allow her to dictate the situation. He got to the heart of the matter. It was not a time for directing but for listening. Mary had humbled herself to hear what Jesus had to say, while Martha was **telling** Jesus what to do. Martha **thought** she was right, but her heart was wrong. Mary's behaviour looked wrong, but her heart was right, and it is the heart God looks at.

Assertive, manipulative people have a very difficult time listening, being still. Their personalities are frantic, always doing something, making things happen, being on top of the situation, looking good. Martha looked good, but it was only in appearance. Jesus' words cut right through the exterior and exposed the symptoms beneath the 'in charge woman'.

*'But Martha was distracted with much serving...'*[1] She was distracted, worried and troubled. The distraction was her job, and assertive people are good at their jobs, only to Martha the job was all important; more important than people, more important than living, more important than Jesus. Here was a once-in-a-lifetime opportunity to talk to God in her own home, and what was more important? Cooking food! All with good intention, but it was all for self. Mary was at Jesus' feet. Martha wanted Jesus at her feet.

Mary must have felt very secure when Jesus came to her rescue, not because He loved her more but because Mary was in the Spirit and Martha was in the flesh, worried and troubled.

Being a controlling, manipulating person produces worry and trouble. Such a person feels every detail has to be in place and all information has to be at the tip of their finger. Martha's plans were coming apart at the seams. Her image was at stake as well as her reputation. Thus the worry and trouble were symptomatic of a deeper problem – insecurity and unbelief.

Why do people feel they must control and manipulate? It is because they do not believe God can manage it. Faith is trusting in God. Control and manipulation is trusting in **self**. Mary was expressing her faith by sitting at Jesus' feet and listening. Martha was exhibiting her unbelief by directing and demanding. Mary was not responding to Martha's request, so Martha asked Jesus to get Mary to do what she wanted. That is manipulation. Jesus, however, only did what the Father told Him to do, not what people wanted Him to do, which is our safeguard against being controlled and manipulated. Mary remained free by following Jesus, and Jesus remained free by following the Father. This is why Martha was worried and troubled. She had nobody to boss around. She was alone, and she was confronted.

This was a mirror for Martha to look at herself. She stood exposed for a moment of time by the light of Jesus' words. Then in John we see Martha's self-exposed even further as Jesus raises Lazarus from the dead.

**Footnotes**

1.   Luke 10:40–41 (NIV)

# *Chapter 11*

# When Manipulators Are Right

The second view we get of Martha is at the grave site of Lazarus.

*'Now a man named Lazarus was sick. He was from Bethany, the village of Mary and her sister Martha. This Mary, whose brother Lazarus now lay sick, was the same one who poured perfume on the Lord and wiped his feet with her hair. So the sisters sent word to Jesus, "Lord, the one you love is sick."*

*When he heard this, Jesus said, "This sickness will not end in death. No, it is for God's glory so that God's Son may be glorified through it." Jesus loved Martha and her sister and Lazarus. Yet when he heard that Lazarus was sick, he stayed where he was two more days. Then he said to his disciples, "Let us go back to Judea."*

*"But Rabbi," they said, "a short while ago the Jews tried to stone you, and yet you are going back there?"*

*Jesus answered, "Are there not twelve hours of daylight? A man who walks by day will not stumble, for he sees by this world's light. It is when he walks by night that he stumbles, for he has no light."*

*After he had said this, he went on to tell them, "Our friend Lazarus has fallen asleep; but I am going there to wake him up."*

*His disciples replied, "Lord, if he sleeps, he will get better." Jesus had been speaking of his death, but his disciples thought he meant natural sleep.*

*So then he told them plainly, "Lazarus is dead, and for your sake I am glad I was not there, so that you may believe. But let us go to him."*

*Then Thomas (called Didymus) said to the rest of the disciples, "Let us also go, that we may die with him."*

*On his arrival, Jesus found that Lazarus had already been in the tomb for four days. Bethany was less than two miles from Jerusalem, and many Jews had come to Martha and Mary to comfort them in the loss of their brother. When Martha heard that Jesus was coming, she went out to meet him, but Mary stayed at home.*

*"Lord," Martha said to Jesus, "if you had been here, my brother would not have died. But I know that even now God will give you whatever you ask."*

*Jesus said to her, "Your brother will rise again."*

*Martha answered, "I know he will rise again in the resurrection at the last day."*

*Jesus said to her, "I am the resurrection and the life. He who believes in me will live, even though he dies; and whoever lives and believes in me will never die. Do you believe this?"*

*"Yes, Lord," she told him, "I believe that you are the Christ, the Son of God who has come into the world."*

*And after she had said this, she went back and*

*called her sister Mary aside. "The Teacher is here,"*
*she said, "and is asking for you." When Mary heard*
*this, she got up quickly and went to him. Now Jesus*
*had not yet entered the village, but was still at the place*
*where Martha had met him. When the Jews who had*
*been with Mary in the house, comforting her, noticed*
*how quickly she got up and went out, they followed*
*her, supposing she was going to the tomb to mourn*
*there.*

*When Mary reached the place where Jesus was and*
*saw him, she fell at his feet and said, "Lord, if you*
*had been here, my brother would not have died."*

*When Jesus saw her weeping, and the Jews who had*
*come along with her also weeping, he was deeply*
*moved in spirit and troubled. "Where have you laid*
*him?" he asked.*

*"Come and see, Lord," they replied.*

*Jesus wept.*

*Then the Jews said, "See how he loved him!"*

*But some of them said, "Could not he who opened*
*the eyes of the blind man have kept this man from*
*dying?"*

*Jesus, once more deeply moved, came to the tomb.*
*It was a cave with a stone laid across the entrance.*
*"Take away the stone," he said.*

*"But, Lord," said Martha, the sister of the dead*
*man, "by this time there is a bad odour, for he has*
*been there four days."*

*Then Jesus said, "Did I not tell you that if you*
*believed, you would see the glory of God?"*

*So they took away the stone. Then Jesus looked up*
*and said, "Father, I thank you that you heard me. I*
*knew that you always hear me, but I said this for the*

> benefit of the people standing here, that they may
> believe that you sent me."
>
> When he had said this, Jesus called in a loud voice,
> "Lazarus, come out!" The dead man came out, his
> hands and feet wrapped with strips of linen, and a
> cloth around his face. Jesus said to them, "Take off
> the grave clothes and let him go."'

Assertive, controlling people are not easy to get along with. The Marys of this world are much easier to love. Yet Jesus loved both Martha and Mary. And His love for Martha did not alter His obedience to the Father. It enabled Jesus to confront her with the truth.

Both Martha and Mary sent a prayer request to Jesus to come and heal their brother, Lazarus, whom Jesus loved. They wanted Jesus to come immediately but He did not. He stayed where He was for two more days.

I do not think this settled well with Martha. Jesus, for a second time, had not done what she had asked, and as a result Lazarus had died! This time Martha was clearly in the right and Jesus was wrong. The body of Lazarus was dead proof of that.

There is nothing more irritating than a manipulator being right. They will drive their point home until you acknowledge their rightness and your wrongness. They take advantage of these incidents and use them to prove their position.

I remember reading a poster that said, 'Some people think we are conceited, but we know we are perfect.' This is the height of self-exultation which is contrary to everything Christ teaches.

Martha was now right and about to make her point, for as soon as Jesus appeared, Martha came running and said,

'*Lord, if You had been here, my brother would not have died.*'[1] Martha was blaming Jesus for her brother's death. She was attempting to put a guilt trip on Him. Why was it Jesus' fault? Why was it anybody's fault? For Martha it had to be somebody's fault because what happened to Lazarus was not in her plan, not in her control.

Martha had a plan. She knew how this tragedy could have been prevented, but Jesus once again did not listen to her. And because Jesus did not snap to it, Lazarus died. It never occurred to her that it could have been her fault. But then again, the Marthas of this world are not good at being honest with themselves. They must find a scapegoat to appease their sense of rightness.

Do not get me wrong, Martha was not a malfunctioning church member who lived in rebellion. She was a spiritual woman who loved Jesus, gave to His ministry, ministered to His needs and sacrificed much for Him. It was simply this area of her personality that was ruled by the flesh that gave her problems. It was her blindspot.

In many ways the Marthas of this world are productive, insightful and good people. They just have not yet died to these areas of self. Since they often get so much done they have not yet learned to rely fully on the Spirit to build the Kingdom of God.

Martha, like many of these multi-talented, self-righteous people, is a tiger held by the tail. You cannot live without them, and yet you cannot live with them. It takes a Spirit-guided wisdom to handle them. In Jesus Martha had met her match.

Imagine you are a pastor and Martha is a member of your church. She calls you to come and pray the prayer of faith for her brother who is very ill. But God tells you to wait four days, so when you do show up she is waiting and her brother is dead. What would you expect to hear from the Devil or from Martha? 'What kind of pastor are you, coming after my brother has died? You don't even care about your sheep! You irresponsible, ungrateful hypocrite!' Do you think Martha would ever give to that church again? Do you think she would talk to others about you? The answers are obvious.

Very often controlling people pressure you to compromise God's Word, to do their will and not God's will. Jesus had to let Lazarus die, knowing what somebody like Martha would think and say. Yet Jesus chose to follow the Father, and so must we.

If we live to please the expectations of the Marthas then we are living for self. Jesus could have gone and healed Lazarus to meet the image of what everybody thought a good pastor should do. But He did not. Jesus came in response to their faith, for they did believe Jesus could and would heal Lazarus, but Jesus did not respond to Martha or Mary's **way of faith**.

Martha's guilt trip was, 'You missed it because You did not do it my way.' But Jesus came against her guilt trip with His **truth**:

> *'I am the resurrection and the life. He who believes in Me, though he may die, he shall live. And whoever lives and believes in Me will never die. **Do you believe this?**'*[2]

This again is the heart of the issue – do you believe? Not in your way, not in your ability to fix things, but do you believe in **Me?** Her moment came again: Do you believe in God's ability or in your own ability?

The responsibility for Lazarus' death which Martha

attempted to place on Jesus was now thrown back on her. She was no match for Jesus. The Spirit will always conquer the flesh.

Again in a vulnerable spot, that uncomfortable zone for controlling people, her response was classic. Did she admit she was wrong? No! Did she apologise for falsely accusing Jesus of being responsible for the death of Lazarus? No! Did she ask Jesus for help to believe? No! She manoeuvred her way out of the conversation. She said, *'Yes, Lord, I believe that You are the Christ, the Son of God, who is to come into the world.'*[3]

Her flesh was working overtime. It was a brilliant answer but to the wrong question. She boldly proclaimed she believed, but in a different issue. And then we read, *'And when she had said these things, she went her way...'*[4]

Martha excused herself from her confrontation with the truth. She still did not face the issue of trusting in her ability to see Lazarus healed God's way. It is very much like a church member telling the pastor at the end of a service that it was a great sermon but then walking out the door continuing to do what they wanted to do anyway.

It is here that we must realise that acknowledgement is not the same as repentance. Martha acknowledged that Jesus was God. Martha acknowledged she believed, but not for the purpose of changing. She acknowledged who Jesus was to suit herself. Her statement was a means to deflect the spotlight off her and back on to Jesus. It was a highly developed defence mechanism to protect self. It is a strategy used by many manipulative people. They say what people like to hear.

Secondly, revelation is not synonymous with change. People like Martha generally have the perceptive ability to receive revelation from God, but acting upon the Word or repenting very often does not follow. This again is deceptive because these people appear to understand and yet continue in their own ways. Martha did not want to pick up her cross and follow Jesus. She threw it down and ran.

When Mary came to Jesus she said the same thing as Martha: *'Lord, if You had been here, my brother would not have died.'*[5] But Jesus responded quite differently than He did to Martha. Instead of confronting her for unbelief He began to weep. Why was this? Because the spirit in which Mary expressed her grief was quite different from the spirit in which Martha accused Jesus of neglect. And here lies the enigmatic problem with controlling people: They can say the same thing, do the same thing, but the spirit in which they do it is entirely different. Putting your finger on the problem is like handling a snake. They slither around like Martha did, never quite answering the questions, changing the subject, pointing out other faults and speaking half-truths.

One of the main difficulties we face when dealing with people who intimidate, control and manipulate us is **motive**. Many times their behaviour and words seem right, but their motive is wrong. They are doing it for self gain rather than for the other person's growth. This was the issue Jesus exposed in Martha.

Martha's self-life rose up again as Jesus reached the tomb and shouted out, *'Take away the stone.'*[6] Out of all the people standing around, who spoke up, but Martha? Out of all the spectators, look who was still trying to take charge, Martha. And look who thought she still knew more than God – Martha! She called out, *'Lord, by this time there is a stench, for he has been dead four days.'*[7]

Again Jesus confronts her unbelief by saying, *'Did I not*

*say to you that if you would believe you would see the glory of God?'*[8] To this she did not answer; no record of repentance. She was one tough lady. She refused to face her motives.

We see Martha again in John 12:2 where, as before, she is still serving the Lord food and Mary is on her knees pouring costly oil on His feet. Martha is still standing in self-ability, Mary is still bowing in humility.

Mary had successfully learned to live with her sister Martha, a strong, directive do-it-my-way-lady. Mary's secret was in walking in obedience to Christ first, and this kept her free from the control of her sister.

Helping intimidators change is admittedly no picnic. It takes confrontation, patience, love and faith. As much as Jesus confronted the Pharisees they never did admit to their sin. Still others did, like Peter, Moses, Gideon, Paul and possibly Martha. She may even have been one of the one hundred and twenty who were filled with the Holy Spirit on the day of Pentecost. Her repentance was her key into that blessed chamber of Holy fire. Did she make that choice?

## Footnotes

1. John 11:21 (NKJV)
2. John 11:25–26 (NKJV)
3. John 11:27 (NKJV)
4. John 11:28 (NKJV)
5. John 11:32 (NKJV)
6. John 11:39 (NKJV)
7. John 11:39 (NKJV)
8. John 11:40 (NKJV)

# Chapter 12

# A Further Look at the Intimidator

Christians who manipulate, intimidate and control often misinterpret their circumstances. These individuals are very good at getting their own way and making things happen for their advantage. This circumstantial evidence often leads them to believe that they are living by faith and that God is answering their prayers.

It was God's will that Jacob, the second-born child, received the birthright, but his method of accomplishing this was manipulative and destructive. The mother of James and John knew Jesus had promised her two sons a special place in His Kingdom, and she was going to ensure that they got it by being the first to ask. These people prayed, but then they pushed, manipulated and forced things to happen. When it did happen they rejoiced that God answered **their** prayers. They were then all the more convinced they were in God's will, when in reality they were deceived and disobedient. They were walking in a counterfeit faith. Jesus said,

> 'The lamp of the body is the eye. Therefore, when the eye is good, your whole body also is full of light. But when your eye is bad, your body also is full of

*darkness. Therefore take heed that the light which is in you is not darkness. If then your whole body is full of light, having no part dark, the whole body will be full of light, as when the bright shining of a lamp gives you light.'*[1]

These people have wrong motives. Their oversized egos will not allow them to be wrong. They then use circumstances to justify their desires or to validate their spirituality. The Corinthians were also living in this egotistical deception. They were moving in the gifts of the Spirit, led by the best – Paul, Peter and Apollos – and they had experienced the supernatural. Yet in the end they were babies thinking they were men. They were carnal believing they were spiritual. They were in need of repentance thinking they were righteous.

The Corinthian Christians were deceived by the outward display of gifts and had forgotten the heart. The motive is God's first concern. So full of pride had they become that they were even questioning the authority and apostleship of Paul.

Unfortunately for them, things did not always go their way. Intimidators are self-servers, and when everything falls into place for them they are even harder to live with. James gives us some insight into this enigma in chapter 3:14:

*'But if you have bitter envy and self-seeking in your hearts, do not boast and lie against the truth. This wisdom does not descend from above, but is earthly, sensual, **demonic**. For where envy and **self-seeking** exist, confusion and every evil thing will be there.'*

Where manipulators, controllers and intimidators operate, confusion and uneasiness follow. Most cannot put their finger on **why** they feel used or on edge, but there is an inexplicable repulsion when around these kinds of people.

People who are intimidators can cross the line from being in the flesh to behaving under the influence of evil spirits. Self-exhibition is a potential door for the demonic. Saul slowly sank from being an anointed leader to a man in the flesh greedy for position, to an oppressed, demonized person. His desire to retain control and image eventually led to his demise.

The whole lure surrounding the occult is in obtaining power to control others. It is the extreme side of manipulation and intimidation. Jesus is the fountainhead of freedom, Satan is the source of domination. John tells us that:

> '... *the whole world lies **under** the **sway** of the wicked one.*'[2]

Paul wrote,

> '... *in which you once walked according to the course of this world, according to the prince of the power of the air, the spirit who now works in the sons of disobedience.*'[3]

The thirst for control is spearheaded by Satan.

Like Saul, intimidators can end up with a wrong spirit. Their words may sound spiritual, their behaviour in church will look the same as others, but they are of a different spirit. They will not receive correction. They are more concerned with the law than with grace. They tend to shift from one argument to another, changing the subject and placing blame on other people. They can appear spiritual and often make capable leaders. They are generally good at organizing and motivating people. They fixate on minor points and know how to make themselves scarce when they are not functioning at peak levels. And finally, they are critical of others and their organization.

In contrast to this, God's wisdom produces fruit that is pure, peaceable, gentle, willing to yield, full of mercy and goodness, without partiality and without hypocrisy. People with this kind of spirit are easy to be around. One can relax and share openly with them. But if you find yourself afraid to share with someone or become secretive when you are with them, it is a good indication that you are dealing with a manipulative person.

Intimidators are also hypocrites. Their public life appears all together but their private life is shrouded in secrecy. They can glad-hand those in authority over them, while dominating those under them. They will be personable with people in leadership but cold to their friends and family. They love to know everything about you but you know nothing about them.

Jesus gives us God's answer for change:

'*God resists the proud, but gives grace to the humble.*'[4]

Therefore,

'***Humble*** *yourselves in the sight of the Lord, and He will lift you up.*'[5]

Humility is the key to the Kingdom of God. It simply

means coming to terms with the way we really are. It is knowing who God is and who we are, as well as recognising the value of others around us.

Humility is being willing to serve and to be served, to lift up others around us and to aim for God's approval, not man's. Humility does not have to prove it is worthy. It can turn the other cheek when misunderstood, go the extra mile when there is nothing in it for self. Humility will bless those who have cursed it, do good to those who hate it, pray for those who spitefully use it. Humility is the opposite of control. It is surrender to God.

Intimidators find it hard to submit to authority, particularly when they see no personal gain in it. But humility founded in love for Christ will say, as did Shadrach, Meshach and Abed-Nego: *'Whether God delivers us or not, we will not bow down to your image.'* They were not serving God for what they could get but for what they could **give**. Dying we live, giving we receive, forgiving we are pardoned, bowing down we are raised up, carrying the cross we are free. Change is possible:

> *'If anyone desires to come after Me, let him deny himself, and take up his cross, and follow Me.'*[6]

### Footnotes
1.  Luke 11:34–36 (NKJV)
2.  1 John 5:19 (NKJV)
3.  Ephesians 2:2 (NKJV)
4.  James 4:6 (NKJV)
5.  James 4:10 (NKJV)
6.  Matthew 16:24 (NKJV)

# PART III

## Who is Winning –
## Victim or Victor?

# You Better Watch Out!

It is very easy to look at the intimidators and assign all blame to them. Their behaviour is more apparent. Yet we have seen how both intimidator and intimidatee need to change. In Part III we explore how both kinds of people work together to keep the facade, and how to discover the road to freedom.

Winston S. Churchill said, 'An appeaser is one who feeds a crocodile, hoping it will eat him last!'

The well known song of the intimidator is:

'You better watch out, you better not cry.
You better not pout, I'm telling you why –
Santa Claus is coming to town.
He's making a list, and checking it twice.
Gonna find out who's naughty or nice.
Santa Claus is coming to town.'

How the intimidator and intimidatee work, live or relate to each other is a complex interchange. The surprise is, they are more alike than we would want to admit.

# Chapter 13

## Profile of an Intimidator and Intimidatee

I knew of a husband and wife who lived a secret life of master and slave. The husband was an executive in a prominent business who was excessively concerned about his image. He continually threatened to divorce his wife if she did not do as he wanted. There were frequent warnings never to expose their marital difficulties because he assured her he could prove they were all her fault, and she would therefore only bring disgrace upon herself.

In public he constantly corrected her and took over situations if he felt she was not performing up to his standard. He was domineering and psychologically bullying to press her into the mould of a slave.

She, on the other hand, always felt inferior to his linguistic abilities. He would out-smart, out-reason and out-verbalise her. She either lost or gave up in most of their arguments.

He was an excellent provider. They had a comfortable life. Even though he controlled most of the money, she nonetheless had most of what she wanted in the material realm.

To be around this Christian couple could only be described as incredulous, outrageous, heartbreaking! He was dominating, controlling and manipulative, and sadly he did it all with a smile in the name of the Lord. He was only concerned with image, and her whole game was fear and compromise.

Whose fault was it? Both of them. She was allowing his sin to rule the house just to keep the peace and not incur the wrath of her husband. She was afraid to confront. She had compromised the truth and did not believe God's Word. She was a coward and would not face up to her own fears and insecurities.

He did not love his wife as Christ loved the Church. None of the fruits of the Spirit were evident in his behaviour – love, joy, peace, longsuffering, kindness, goodness, faithfulness, gentleness and self control. He was walking in the flesh and using another human being for his own selfish ends while he twisted biblical submission around her neck like a noose.

It was the classic story of beauty and the beast. He was the beast in everybody's eyes, and she was the poor, suffering beauty who so lovingly endured the treatment of her husband. Yet her beauty was only skin deep, for her heart was full of compromise, fear, cowardice, unbelief, disobedience and unforgiveness.

If she believed in God's Word, she could bring God's salvation into both of their lives, but her compromising heart forced her to live within the lie.

So many in co-dependent Christian relationships believe they are suffering for Christ. In reality they are in bondage. Very often this stems from misunderstanding the Scriptures. When Peter and Paul wrote about suffering, it was in the context of relationships between non-believers and believers, not believers and believers.

For a believing wife to submit to a believing husband

who is abusing his authority through intimidation, threats, verbal lashing or anger is ungodly submission. By remaining silent she becomes party to his sin. They are in an unholy league together. The key to breaking this co-dependent relationship is **exposure**. Sin must be confessed before it can be forgiven. As long as the wife hides it she is as much to blame as the husband. They are **both** keeping the light out of their marriage and living in the darkness of secrecy.

Jesus said,

> *'And this is the condemnation, that the light has come into the world, and men loved darkness rather than light, because their deeds were evil.'*[1]

People like darkness because it hides their sins and weakness. Exposure to the Light is the answer which will bring healing, deliverance and wholeness.

There may even seem to be legitimate reasons for keeping the husband's behaviour hidden, such as not wanting to bring shame, disgrace, possible loss of job or position in the church. But all these reasons are only **flesh**. They are attempting to protect self which needs to be exposed to the light. Jesus crucified self. It is not worth protecting, saving, hiding or preserving. Therefore, the wife who thinks she is suffering for the Gospel, is in reality partnering with the enemy to maintain her husband's self-life and her own.

In the guise of love she is hiding her fear. What is called for is tough love, which is 'walking in the light'. Tough love is 'speaking the truth in love'; it is straight and direct, leaving no room for misinterpretation, because when grey areas are allowed, the truth is easily avoidable. Jesus demonstrated this tough love by exposing the hypocrisy of the Pharisees and the self-life of His disciples. He called all people to come to grips with the truth before they jeopardized their lives. Jesus was more concerned about them than He was about how they responded to Him.

This is where the cross intersects our lives. The one thing an intimidatee fears the most is confronting the intimidator, and the one thing an intimidator despises is being confronted. Yet all of us need to be confronted with our sin, which is exactly what Jesus did on the cross. Imagine Jesus saying to His disciples, 'I have been thinking about the political and social situation of Israel, and I feel because of its instability this may not be a good time to rock the boat. Let us just keep the peace and attempt to blend in to society. Speaking the truth would upset most people.'

That would be unthinkable! But the intimidated wife is willing to live the lie in order to keep the peace. She has not realised that the well-being of her husband is more important than her peaceful status quo. Jesus spoke the truth knowing it would cost Him His life because He esteemed us of greater value than Himself.

This deception has kept many relationships in bondage because secrecy is the Devil's game. Just as the wife can contribute to the problem, she can also be the very key to deliverance in the relationship, if she is willing to confront the intimidator, her Goliath, and to bring the sin out into the light. In a single bound she can go from being victim to deliverer.

False submission brings subjugation. True submission brings liberation. This woman wanted to be a good Christian wife thinking that the way to love her husband was to live under his thumb and submit to his every whim. But this in turn only reinforced her husband's controlling behaviour.

Many spouses who subject themselves to spiritual machismo and Christian chauvinism do not understand the behaviour of love. They think that if they just love the other person enough everything will change. But how does love behave? Jesus said, *'If you love me, you will obey what I command.'*[2]

So the question comes: Is this wife obeying the **Lord** when she submits to her husband? The answer is **NO!** She is living in fear and we are commanded to live in faith. She is giving in to preserve her self-life (her image, her dignity, her comfortable world), and Jesus said it must be crucified. She compromises when she does not help her husband become a godly man by confronting his selfish behaviour.

Through his intimidation the husband slowly bends his wife's heart away from following Christ and on to following **him**. He becomes the interpretation of God's Word, he becomes the source of supply, he becomes the one to obey, he becomes her god. She bows to his wishes out of fear rather than bowing to Christ out of love. Both are Christians, but each interprets God's Word for their own personal gain. Very often intimidators are Bible-bashers, quoting scriptures out of context, demanding allegiance and threatening hell. Intimidatees seem to find scriptures that legitimise their compromise.

Freedom will only come as each obeys Christ first and stops protecting self.

## Footnotes

1. John 3:19 (NKJV)
2. John 14:15 (NIV)

# *Chapter 14*

## The Hidden Truth

The Pharisees, scribes and priests in Jesus' time were religious intimidators. They held people in bondage through spiritual blackmail. From all appearances it looked like the masses were enslaved because of the consequences imposed upon them by the religious hierarchy. But what the victims of the super spiritual elitism did not know was that their intimidators were also in bondage. There is a well kept secret hidden by the intimidator from the intimidatee: The intimidator is afraid of the intimidatee.

Several times throughout the four Gospels it is recorded, *'And the chief priests and the scribes sought how they might kill Him, **for they feared the people.***'[1] Those Pharisees lived in fear that the masses would one day wake up and realise that they did not have to obey their ungodly spiritual leaders. They were wrong to follow them or listen to them; they could find God without them. All the religious leaders' powers came from the lie, 'I know something you don't know.' This was the hidden truth about Saul when he was intimidating David, he did it **only** because he was **afraid of David**. Saul the intimidator was intimidated.

The Pharisees presented an image of confidence and unruffled composure, but it was all an illusion. They were filled with insecurity. This is the intimidator's trump card, an elaborately developed defence mechanism for avoiding the truth of their own cowardice while speaking lies through an image of superiority. Goliath trusted in his size and armour. The Pharisees used the law and ecclesiastical hocus-pocus. Others use anger, guilt trips, passivity or money.

Jesus was not intimidated by the scribes because His security was not in their approval but in the Father's acceptance. Therefore Jesus was not only a threat to them, but He was also their key to freedom. Jesus came to seek and to save the lost which included them. The Pharisees, like all others, needed to be confronted with truth. It was tough love they needed if they were going to change. This is the only hope for the intimidator – the truth that sets people free!

The apostle Paul was a brilliant, aggressive, legalistic hot-head who intimidated the religious priests as well as the common man. He stormed through the country waving his legal rights and exercising the strong arm of the law until **truth** confronted him on the road to Damascus. It was there that he 'saw the light'. There is no hope without the light. Jesus said,

> '*And you shall know the **truth**, and the **truth** shall make you free.*'[2]

Paul's salvation was through confrontation with the truth which became his trademark throughout his ministry. Intimidators may seem to be cast in an impenetrable mould, but tough love can break it through.

In many cases it is the victims that are the hardest to change. They have lived with the lie that they are the victims, life is against them, they are stuck with a destiny of being used. Victims have learned to be non-responsible, which makes them unblameable. Therefore, to take action means they run the risk of being account-able. They do not want to be responsible for their part of the relationship.

I knew of an intimidating husband who saw the light and changed from a domineering, intimidating, insensi-tive man to one who was trying to walk in humility and truly care for his wife. The wife, who had been mistreated for a number of years, saw her opportunity to pay him back. She turned into the intimidator. One may be tempted to say that he was finally reaping what he sowed, and in this case it was true. But Christ does not repay us according to our sins. He gives us mercy and grace and He calls us to love as He loves.

The hidden point of this drama lies in the fact that she was always an intimidator, even as the victim of the hus-band's domination, only now under the right circum-stances it became apparent. Like David, it was not the naked body of Bathsheba that caused David to sin, it was the adultery in his heart that found expression under the right conditions. Circumstances do not make us sin. They only reveal what is already in our heart.

So who is the victim and who is the victor? Who is using who? Who is controlling who? Different relationships will have a different mixture, but a little of both is in each of them. Each must face the game they are playing, each is responsible to stop using the other as a crutch. Nobody else is responsible for our emotions or actions. We are all accountable for our responses.

# Footnotes

1.   Luke 22:2 (NKJV)
2.   John 8:32 (NKJV)

# *Chapter 15*

## From Selfishness to Selflessness

Being around a selfish person creates tension. Whether it is the self-pitying victim who uses depression to gain attention, or the intimidator who demands service, the attitude is everything Christ is not, even if the person is a Christian.

Unfortunately psychology has redefined sin as disease or dysfunctional personality, thus providing Christians with an excuse for clinging on to their self-life. The answer is not learning how to live with our dysfunctions but to die to them. The apostle Paul, an aggressive, intelligent, self-disciplined individual (who must have been difficult to live with) learned this principle early on in his Christian life. Single-handedly he was out to eradicate Christianity. He was moving completely in self-power until he encountered Christ on the road to Damascus when he learned his first lesson in humility. He found himself on the ground listening to Jesus. Could you imagine Martha and Paul being married? Not likely, but neither can a person living in the flesh be married to Christ without first dying to self.

Paul was a born leader and was very successful, as long as he was in the world. However, success in Christ is not measured by the abilities of our self-life but by our willingness to die and walk in selflessness. This was the conflict Paul experienced in Romans 7:

> *'For I know that in me (that is, in my flesh) nothing good dwells;* [that was the first revelation Paul received that put him on the road to change] *for to will is present with me, but **how** to perform what is good I do not find.*
>
> *But I see* [praise God he saw] *another law in my members, warring against the law of my mind, and bringing me into captivity to the law of sin which is in my members. O wretched man that I am! Who will deliver me from this body of death?'* [1]

After meeting Christ on the road to Damascus Paul saw his selfishness. The whole reason he was persecuting Christians was to further his own career and prove his self-righteousness. He saw that his whole motivation was wrong. Now the struggle began between Christ and himself. Who would be Lord? Who would be in command? Who would be right?

Paul was wrestling to hold on to his self-life. After all, he was successful, intelligent, highly gifted, a commanding personality. But none of these were under the Lordship of Christ. God was asking him, 'Will you allow Christ to live His life out through you, or will you continue to live your life?'

Paul did come through this battle, for he wrote, *'I thank God – through Jesus Christ **our Lord!'*** [1] He died! **He believed Christ had crucified his old self-life** and started to walk in the newness of life, the life of the Holy Spirit. Now Paul was not living to satisfy self but allowed the Holy Spirit to live the life of Christ out through him for the glory of God, not for his glory.

Paul was still a strong personality, a leader with brilliant capabilities, but he was not living **for self**, protecting self, promoting self. He was living for the glory of God. He was decreasing, Christ was increasing. He had been '... *crucified with Christ*; it (was) no longer [he] who lived, but Christ who lived in (him); and the life which (he) now [lived he lived] by **faith** in the Son of God.'[2]

How did Paul make this transition? **By repenting and believing**. How did Paul die to self? **By faith**. Paul simply **believed** his selfish nature, his self-life, **had been crucified with Christ on the cross**. This is the key for change, for hope, for freedom. Living for self keeps us in bondage. **Believing** we are dead to self liberates us. Paul said,

> '*Now it is not my old self, but Christ himself who lives in me.*'[3]

Other translations say, '*I died when Christ died on the cross...*'; '*Christ took me to the cross with him, and I died there with him...*' In Romans Paul writes, '*...our original humanity was nailed to the cross with Him...*'; '*...be aware of this, that our old self has been jointly crucified with him...*'; '*...so that we are no longer controlled by old habits and attitudes.*'[4]

Whatever you chose to call it, your self-life, old personality, former self, ego, original humanity, sinful nature, it **has been crucified with Christ**, and your ability to be free from it starts with **believing it is true**. Until you believe, you will be captive to your old ways, habits, attitudes, behaviours and sins. Paul said the life he lived now was by **faith**.

This is what Jesus challenged Martha with, '*Do you believe...?*' Do we believe? Why should we protect self if it is already dead? What image is there to preserve if we are dead? There is no other way of being free as a victim or an intimidator. Both must **believe** they are dead in Christ as well as raised to new life in Christ. Paul wrote,

> *'Likewise **you also, reckon** (**consider**) *yourselves to be dead indeed to sin* (self), *but alive to God in Christ Jesus our Lord.'*[5]

God is not talking about changing our circumstances but changing **our nature** so we respond to people and situations entirely differently. Mary was able to live in peace with Martha because she was dead to self, a self that could easily have felt like a victim under Martha's strong personality. When we are alive to self we fall under its bondages, but when we are alive and sensitive to Christ we fall under His freedom.

## Footnotes
1.   Romans 7:25 (NKJV)
2.   Galatians 2:20 (NKJV)
3.   Galatians 2:20 (Norlie Translation)
4.   Romans 6:6 (NKJV, Weymouth, Way 1st, Berkley, Johnson)
5.   Romans 6:11 (NKJV)

# Chapter 16

## Facing Our Cross

Selfish people are generally avoided by the body of Christ because no matter how much you give them it is never enough. There is never enough pleasing for intimidators, never enough sympathy for self-perceived victims, never enough submission for controllers.

Solomon wrote, *'The leech has two daughters – Give and Give!'*[1] Self is a leech, it is never satisfied.

> *'There are three things that are never satisfied, four things never say, "Enough"; the grave, the barren womb, the earth that is not satisfied with water, and the fire, that never says, "It is enough."'*[2]

I would like to add a fifth one: Self also has no end to its consumption. This is why these relationships fail so often, and why others keep away from them.

Yet, if we are willing to see God's higher purpose, these irritating people can become the small stone that forms the pearl in the oyster. The intimidator can be that door to glory for the victim, and the victim can be the path to freedom for the intimidator. God's pure love and selfless-ness can be seen in the face of their selfishness, His grace

in their law, His light in their dark side. But who is the
stone and who is the pearl in these relationships? The
determining factor is who sees God's purpose in the relationship. If the victim decides to change, then God can
actually use the intimidator to help the victim become
more Christlike, or vice versa. God took death and turned
it into a glorious resurrection. What was meant for evil in
Joseph's life, God turned around for good. This process
enables the stone to become a pearl.

In all relationships having the correct perception is vital
to responding with godly contentment. In many of these
relationships two people have come together out of need
or by the subtlety of the Devil.

Is it not ironic that many people say, 'I never want to be
like my parents,' and end up exactly like them? Others
who run away from their intimidating, controlling, self-
pitying parents end up marrying into the same kind of
relationship. Who is drawing these people together? Why
does the curse keep following them? The enemy of our
soul is out to create relationships that are destructive. Yet
even these relationships are redeemable. The more 'need'
we take into a relationship, the greater the risk of failure.
The intimidator who needs to be served and the victim
who needs sympathy are at opposite poles. Each is asking
of the other what each does not want to give because they
are both focused on receiving. And self will not give to
another self unless there is something in it for self.

This is why these types of relationships are so destruc-
tively heart-breaking. Both the intimidator and intimidatee are struggling with all their might to keep their self-
life alive. Neither one realises that the success of the
relationship is in direct relation to their ability to be
selfless towards each other. Self only has room for self,

but a selfless heart makes room for others. This is why God has room for all mankind. He is perfectly selfless. He is pure, divine love. When love is compared to self we can clearly see the problem in all relationships.

Love is patient, kind and gracious.
Self is quick-tempered, demanding and ungracious.
Love always looks for a way to be constructive.
Self looks for ways to keep others under its control.
Love is neither anxious to impress nor envious or boastful.
Self is always seeking to promote its image.
Love is not arrogant, conceited or egotistical. It does not put on airs or cherish inflated ideas of its own importance.
Self does all of the above.
Love is never rude, indecent or selfish. It does not pursue selfish aims.
Self does.
Love bears no malice, never reckons up her wrongs, nor is quick to take offence. It is not irritable or touchy.
Self is brilliant at remembering people's past mistakes.
Love takes no pleasure when others do wrong.
Self secretly smiles because ground is gained for moving up in status and position.
Love is always glad when truth prevails.
Self will avoid any truth that exposes, but will use truth to expose others' faults.
Love overlooks faults and is slow to expose.
Self takes note of the faults of others and likes to expose them.

Love has unquenchable faith.

Self lives in unbelief.

Love can face anything and has no limits to its endurance.

Self will face only what it chooses and endures only as long as there is some personal gain.

Love will never come to an end – it endures forever.

Self will be done away with at Christ's return.[3]

Hope for these relationships is not found in ridding ourselves of these intimidating people, but in beholding Christ in the midst of the relationship. There are times when we must break the threatening intimidation as David did. At other times we must learn to see the beauty in the beast, as Jesus saw a mighty man in Gideon the weak, humility in Peter's machismo, courage in Moses' fears and ultimately resurrection in death. The relationship may have started out with wrong motives, but in Christ it can end in redemptive grace.

We do not have to remain victims or intimidators. Jesus offers us freedom through the cross, that stone in the oyster. Now that we can **see** the kind of relationship we are in, it does not mean we are to dump the other person. God can use the relationship for His glory and for our personal growth. Every time we avoid the process of dying to self and run away from an opportunity to confront our intimidator or intimidatee we put down our cross and remain imprisoned. Taking the stone out of the oyster removes all possible chances for a pearl. We miss many opportunities by remaining selfish, angry, living in unforgiveness or placating our ego. If a person survives through silence in a relationship with a person with an angry personality, the cross is not the anger. It is the silence. Breaking the silence barrier is the daily test of denying self. That person needs to speak the truth in love.

I have had many people come into my office saying, 'Fix them!' These people want me to be God in their relationships. I have learned to do as Jesus did when the man with the sick boy said, '...*if you can do anything, have compassion on us and help us.*'[4] Jesus said, '*If you can believe...*'[5] He placed the responsibility back on the father.

Our job is not to fix people like a mechanic tunes up a car but to help people **see** the **truth** and **act upon it**. Only God can change people.

How do we look at the stone in the oyster? Is it possible for the stone to become a pearl or will it simply remain an irritant to the oyster? The intimidator can become the very door to victory for the victim if the victim will take every opportunity to face themselves and the intimidator. The victim can become the source of freedom for the intimidator if the intimidator will stop controlling and start trusting God. If you are the one who uses depression to control others, **fight it, resist it**. If you tend to fade into nothingness at the slightest hint of confrontation, **fight it, resist it**. This is your moment of glory. This is your cross. Pick it up and carry it. Do not run to counsellors for help to cope with your flesh or with your unbelief. Go to the cross! If despising another person's weakness brings the beast out in you, those weaknesses are not your cross. Your reaction of disgust is the very thing that needs to be faced.

When Jesus faced the cross, Peter tried to keep Christ alive by pulling out his sword to fight. But Jesus said,

> '*Put your sword into the sheath. Shall I not drink the cup which My Father has given Me?*'[6]

Jesus did not fight and struggle. We so often draw our swords and lash out at anybody who would dare to challenge or confront our motives. At the slightest suggestion that we are at fault, out comes our sword ready to chop off confrontational words that get too close to the mark. Jesus is saying, 'Put your swords away and surrender to the Father's will – death to self!'

There are times when destructive relationships are to be broken off, as when David fled from Saul and Moses left Egypt. But most relationships are to be worked out, layer by layer, defect by defect, fear by fear. The easy way is to remove the stone. God's way is to create a pearl.

## Footnotes
1. Proverbs 30:15 (NKJV)
2. Proverbs 30:15–16 (NKJV)
3. 1 Corinthians 13:4–8 (various translations)
4. Mark 9:22 (NKJV)
5. Mark 9:23 (NKJV)
6. John 18:11 (NKJV)

# PART IV

# Stepping Into Freedom

# Heaven on Earth?

Working through difficult relationships is not our idea of
heaven on earth. We try every method known to **man** to
avoid the only true way known to God:

  *'The just shall live by faith.'*

Faith means that we must rely on God and not ourselves.
But many do not discover the glory of faith until they lay
exhausted in the ashes of their broken relationships.

This final section need not be the final frontier, but
rather the beginning of fruitfulness, inner peace and mira-
cles in your life.

During the Ugandan holocaust the leading Archbishop
was killed by Idi Amin's army. Many of his followers were
shot, butchered, raped and stabbed. Yet one of his
Bishops, Festo Kivengere, who could have lived in bitter-
ness, hatred and unforgiveness, took that leap of faith and
forgave. This released God's power into his life and he
was able to write a book called 'I love Idi Amin.' Faith
can and does bring heaven down to earth.

Living by faith is not a pat theological answer to
patronise hurting people. Faith intersects life in the midst
of the agony of failure to bring Christ's redemption into
the here and now.

# Chapter 17

## Faith – A Doorway to Freedom

How can we find freedom from behaving like intimidators or as victims? The only way is to live in our spirit-man and not in our flesh. The problem is that there are areas of unsubmitted flesh in our lives. This was the problem with the Corinthians. They were born again, Spirit-filled and even moved in a number of gifts, but they still behaved carnally; in other words, they were acting like unsaved people. Like non-believers they were allowing their flesh to rule over them. Their soul (the mind, emotions and will) was not submitted to the Spirit. They were saved, they were new creations, but they had not put on the new man. They were not **acting** the way new creations should.

Paul tells us that if we *'walk in the spirit* [we] *will not fulfil the lust of the flesh'*;[1] it is automatic. But if we do intimidate, control, manipulate, or live in fear feeling sorry for ourselves, then we are fulfilling the desires of the flesh.

We are not to feel sorry for ourselves but to believe self is crucified. We are not to draw attention to self but to lose self in Christ. We are not to protect self but to let it die.

Paul makes another comparison between the soulish and the spiritual life in Galatians 5:19–26:

| The Fruit of the *Spirit* is... | The Fruit of the *flesh* is... |
| --- | --- |
| Love | Fear and Intimidation |
| Joy | Depression and Discouragement |
| Peace | Wrath, Worry, Control, Contention |
| Longsuffering | Short-temperedness, Unbelief, Giving Up, Dismissing People as Inconsequential |
| Kindness | Harsh, Punitive, Coarse, Abusive, Cruel, Unrelenting |
| Goodness | Cantankerous, Disagreeable, Rude, Unfriendly, Narrow-minded |
| Faithfulness | Disloyal, Two-faced, Untrustworthy, Gossiping |
| Gentleness | Abrasive, Annoying, Hurtful, Irritating |
| Self-control | Controlled by Irrational Thoughts, Desires or Emotions, Unsubmissive |

People who allow areas of their flesh-life to remain unsubmitted to God will find themselves acting in self-gratifying ways. And their behaviour will not change until they believe they are no longer in the flesh but in the Spirit. Faith will swing Christians into the Spirit. Doubt will move them back into the flesh. Faith moved Moses, Gideon, Paul, Mary and Peter into victory. Doubt kept Saul and Martha in bondage.

When you are in the flesh you do not know **how** to stop yourself from behaving the same old way. That is because when you are in the flesh you cannot change. The flesh is opposed to the spirit and the spirit to the flesh. The object is not trying to change the flesh, but moving out of the flesh and into the Spirit.

People who act out of their flesh-life feel they can never change, and even if they want to change, they do not know how. Eventually they come to the conclusion that they are trapped. They will say, 'That is just the way I am,' or 'I have tried everything and nothing has worked,' or 'I do not know what else to do.' These people have not yet realised that as long as they live in the flesh they will never change and **cannot** change.

The doorway to change is to **believe** that the intimidator or victim has died in Christ. That person is no more. Various translations of Romans 6:6 say,

> '...*our original humanity, our old self, our old personality, our earlier self, our old inherited self, our former self, our former evil identities, our old sinful self was crucified, wiped out, made ineffective and inactive for evil, was nailed to the cross with Christ.*'

That intimidator, that victim, was nailed to the cross

with Christ, then died, was buried and forever left in the
tomb. A new man arose with Christ as a new person,
which is why Paul wrote,

> *'Now it is not my old self, but Christ Himself who lives
> in me.'*[2]

Faith releases Christ, doubt releases flesh. Therefore
the only way to behave differently is to believe we **are new
creatures in Christ**. Once we truly know **who** we are, then
we will know how to behave. By walking in the Spirit, we
**will** act in love, joy, peace, longsuffering, kindness, goodness, faithfulness, gentleness and self-control.

The moment we walk in the Spirit we are free from the
dictates of the flesh. They still exist, we may feel them,
but we can stand looking at them from our position of
faith saying, 'I am dead to you,' or 'I am non-responsive
to you, and I am alive to God.' This means we want to do
what God wants and not what self wants.

The same process works in the opposite way. When we
are walking in self, we can sense the conviction of the
Spirit, the prick of our conscience, the stirring of God's
voice in our hearts, but we ignore it as though we are dead
to God's call to repent.

As long as we believe we are prisoners to our self, our
past, our feelings, passions and thoughts, then we will
give in to them. But when we believe what Paul wrote,

> *'And those who are Christ's have crucified the flesh
> with its passions and desires,'*[3]

we can walk in freedom.

Faith enables you to resist fear, pity, intimidation and

the desire to control. To act on those is to sow to the flesh, which reaps corruption. Yet to say, 'I am dead to those' is to sow to the spirit and to reap everlasting life.

Many times we miss it by waiting to feel different before we act differently. But that is not faith. Faith obeys God's Word, regardless of the feelings. It takes that first step of faith that seems so awkward. But walking by faith is the door to releasing God into our lives.

For example, as an intimidator you may feel harsh toward another person. What will you do with that human emotion? The Spirit would call for kindness, which means to show goodness in actions, sweetness of disposition, gentleness in communication, benevolence, kindness, affability. Kindness means the ability to act for the welfare of those taxing your patience. This could only happen if the intimidator acts in response to the Spirit and not to self. Every time we act in the Spirit we give the Holy Spirit license to remove abrasive qualities within our character and establish godly behaviour, but we must choose!

It is very much like driving towards a destination. The further you drive on the right road, the closer you get to your journey's end. But the more you drive in the wrong direction, the further you get from your intended goal. Every time you act out of self, you only reinforce the habits of flesh and selfishness and go further and further astray. You must **stop**, **turn around** and move in the Spirit. But there is a major stumbling block to this turning around, and it is fear.

## Footnotes

1.  Galatians 5:16 (NKJV)
2.  Galatians 2:20 (NKJV)
3.  Galatians 5:24 (NKJV)

# Chapter 18

## Fear – The Binding Cord

Fear is the rope that is interwoven among the strands of intimidation, co-dependency and control. It is the cord that binds them together and chains its victims. Whether it is the secret police, the Gestapo, a dictatorial spouse, relative or some other person, these all use fear as a noose around people's necks threatening dire consequences if they do not cooperate.

God asked Israel a question in Isaiah 51:12:

> *'Who are you that you should be afraid of a man who will die, and of the son of a man who will be made like grass?'*

This was indeed a very odd question because Israel at this time was a nation living in captivity. They had been conquered by the Babylonians who had destroyed their homeland, burned their cities, separated their families, killed many men, stolen all their belongings and driven the Israelites into slavery in a foreign country. They were suffering all the ravages of war, the sorrow of humiliation, the loss of family and friends, of country and home. And in this situation God asked, **'Why are you afraid?'**

Why were God's people afraid of the strong? Why are the strong afraid of the weak? Why are husbands afraid of wives and wives afraid of husbands, parents afraid of children, children of parents? The answer is easy: Their threats and behaviour frighten us. Their words and gestures scare us. Their attitude, their helplessness, their tone of voice, their eyes, their pitiful weaknesses make us shudder with fear. The victim is afraid of the intimidator's pressure, the intimidator is afraid of the victim's potential rebellion, and God says 'Why?'

Fear seems so natural to mankind. It is a part of everybody's emotional life. Yet God exposes the fallacy that fear is universal and therefore acceptable. God is announcing, 'You do not have to live in fear!'

Whether fear is psychologically packaged in anxiety, stress, worry, tension, nervousness, shyness, or neurosis, we can be free of it, even if the other person does not change.

Abigail was a '...*woman of good understanding and beautiful appearance,*' but her husband, Nabal, '...*was harsh and evil in his doings.*'[1] How these two came to be married we do not know, but they were like positive and negative – not what we would call a match made in heaven!

As we read of Abigail's attempt to save her husband, her servants and David from making a foolish mistake, we discover that the dominance of her husband did not stop her from acting in faith and growing in Christ. She did not allow this intimidating, harsh, evil man to immobilize, depress, discourage or overcome her. Rather she overcame evil with good.

The story states that David asked Nabal for some food in return for David's protection of Nabal's livestock.

Nabal responded harshly, shamed David's men and was therefore about to be killed as David vowed revenge. Abigail intercepted David with food, godly advice and humility, thus turning away David's anger and saving her household.

Abigail moved in faith, forgiveness and foresight. Had she moved in fear, then death and sorrow would have been the result. Abigail knew her husband was a scoundrel. She admitted that to David when she met him. She was not blind to her husband's faults, nor did she attempt to gloss over them with surrealistic love that pretends all is well when a cancer is growing. Neither did she use her husband as an excuse for her situation. She did not waste her life blaming Nabal for her hardships and sufferings. She moved in faith and not in fear.

Fear would have resigned itself to the situation. Fear would have felt sorry for itself, become quiet and depressed because it felt helpless. This is why the Devil wants Christians to live in fear. It immobilizes them until tragedy takes over. This was the point God was making with Israel: 'Do not blame Babylon for your situation. Look to **Me** and you can still be free, even in the midst of your captivity. Do not allow the threats of your captors to be a noose around your necks.'

Where Abigail succeeded, Adam failed. He allowed the fear of losing his wife to lead him and all of mankind into sin. This was the beginning of fear, control and manipulation. Eve, by eating the fruit, wanted to be more than she was. She was dethroning God and enthroning self. She wanted more control! Since Adam did not want to lose Eve, he wanted to control the situation even though he saw the tragedy, and so he ate too. Each took matters into their own hands which is called manipulation. It is attempting to achieve our purposes through self-effort. Fear moved Adam and Eve to satisfy their need for self-worth. But self-worth is only found in Christ. No other person can give that to us. They discovered this reality as they were driven from the presence of God. The secret that needs to be unveiled is that self-effort does not achieve self-worth, but only brings further disappointment and failure.

Intimidators seek worth and self-importance through controlling their victims. Victims search for purpose by being needed. The motive for both is self-centred. This is why actions can be so deceiving. They may look like loving servants, even appear sacrificial, but the source of their motive is all wrong. Adam's action of partaking may have appeared loving to Eve, but in reality it was selfish. Adam **needed** Eve. He knew what loneliness was. He had already searched the entire animal kingdom for a companion but found none, and now that God had created Eve especially for him, from him, Adam did not want to lose her. Adam's motive was for self.

Paul tells us the results of selfish love which attempts to gain worth and happiness through manipulation:

> 'And though I bestow all my goods to feed the poor, and though I give my body to be burned, but have not love (God's love), **it profits me nothing**.'[2]

In the end Adam's selfish love profited him nothing. His fear of losing what he thought gave him meaning and fulfilment cost him everything. Adam and Eve had to learn the hard way that only **God** can give us worth. Faith is the only way out of fear. Use your faith to be free.

## Footnotes

1.  1 Samuel 25:3 (NKJV)
2.  1 Corinthians 13:3 (NKJV)

# Chapter 19

## Fear and Faith

All one must do to join the Devil's camp is to move into
fear. The temptation Satan put before Eve was 'You can
become **more** like God.' On hearing this, Eve became
**afraid** that if she did not eat the fruit, she would not be as
much like God as she could be. Why do people like to
intimidate others? It gives them a sense of power, of
control, of being like God. It is a fear-driven motive. Why
does the victim try to meet every need of the manipulator?
It fulfils their sense of being the saviour. Adam was trying
to be Eve's saviour, but his motive was rooted in fear. Fear
bound Adam and Eve with the cords of death.

God's antidote for Satan's fear is faith:

> 'For by grace you have been **saved** by **faith**, and **not of**
> **yourselves**; it is the **gift of God**.'[1]

Faith takes things out of our hands, out of our **self** and
places them in God's hands. Faith moves us toward God.

After Adam and Eve sinned, Jesus came walking in the
garden asking, '*Adam, where are you?*' To this Adam
replied, '*I heard Your voice in the garden, and I was **afraid**
because I was naked; and I hid myself.*'[2] This is the reason
Satan wants people to live in fear – it causes them to hide

from God, the only One who can help them. Fear cuts man off from his source of purpose, worth and life, so man only has self to rely on.

The way back to God is by faith:

> '...*let us draw near with a true heart in full assurance of faith, having our hearts sprinkled from an evil conscience and our bodies washed with pure water...*'[3]

Trusting God means laying down our weapons of control, manipulation, intimidation, self-promotion and self-effort and looking to Christ for answers, letting Him resolve the issues. Trying to make things happen because you are afraid they will not work without your intervention leads to an illusion of self-importance. This was Eve's fantasy. She believed the lie that she would be inferior and powerless if she **did not do something about it**. She did not understand as Eleanor Roosevelt so aptly stated, 'No-one can make you feel inferior without your consent.' Neither Satan nor people can put us in our place all by themselves. We first choose to go there. Eve chose, Adam chose and we choose daily to operate in faith or fear.

The words people speak identify whether they are in faith or in fear. The intimidator will say, 'You are always causing trouble. You are so stupid! You are always doing this! I have had to forgive you so often. I will never understand you.' They are always blaming the others. They are afraid to face themselves. The manipulator will say, 'You do not love me anymore. You will make me cry. You have really hurt me now.' They are also blaming other people. Fear keeps them from looking at themselves. When Jesus confronted Adam, Adam's response was to blame his wife. When Jesus confronted Eve, she blamed the Devil, when Jesus got to Satan there was no-one left to blame.

These words of blame exposed their fear. Words of faith will lead to repentance, speaking the truth. Words of the timid victim who is afraid of confrontation sound like, 'Everything is fine. It will be alright soon. It really does not matter. Let's not argue. I give in. Well, praise the Lord anyway, we are so happy, aren't we?' These are words from a heart that is afraid of facing the real issues.

Adam's words were very telling. He said to Jesus,

> *'The woman whom **you** gave to be with me, **she** gave me of the tree, and I ate.'*[4]

Adam was fearful of admitting his guilt because speaking the truth would have exposed the lie he was now believing, namely that his wife was his new source of happiness and meaning. To admit he was wrong would have shattered his new-found sense of worth. Those words locked Adam and Eve in unforgiveness.

When Joshua and the Israelites were about to enter the promised land, God said to Joshua,

> *'Have I not **commanded** you? Be strong and of good courage; do **not be afraid**, nor be dismayed, for the Lord your God is with you wherever you go.'*[5]

Joshua was **commanded not to fear**. This means fear or faith is a choice, not a feeling. Continually throughout the four Gospels Jesus says, 'Believe!' For Joshua this was a critical choice because forty years earlier when the ten spies **spoke** out in fear, it caused the entire nation to forfeit the promises of God. God did not want to see the same mistake happen twice, so this time Joshua is commanded to believe and to **speak faith, not fear**. Those ten spies used fear to intimidate millions of people. Now it was time for faith to inspire the people forward.

Fear speaks depression, discouragement, pity and blame. Faith speaks the answers. The woman with the issue of blood said, *'If I just touch His clothes, I will be healed.'*[6] She had been sick twelve years, spent all her money on doctors and was only deteriorating physically. She could have complained, she could have blamed society and the medical profession, but she did not. She moved in faith. The centurion said, *'...only speak the word and my servant shall be healed.'*[7] Jairus said, *'Come and lay Your hands on her, that she may be healed, and she will live.'*[8] They did not allow people, society, sickness or the unknown to move them into fear. They **spoke their faith** and the answers came.

What we say to one another in relationships either entrenches or releases us. Words can be nails in our coffin or life to our soul. Adam blamed Eve, Eve blamed Satan. Their words sealed their doom to live in fear. Therefore God came and said, 'I will be the blame.' And when Jesus said, *'It is finished,'*[9] mankind never had another reason to fear.

## Footnotes

1. Ephesians 2:8 (NKJV)
2. Genesis 3:9–10 (NKJV)
3. Hebrews 10:22 (NKJV)
4  Genesis 3:12 (NKJV)
5. Joshua 1:9 (NKJV)
6. Mark 5:28 (NIV)
7. Matthew 8:8 (NKJV)
8. Mark 5:23 (NKJV)
9. John 19:30 (NKJV)

# *Chapter 20*

## Do I Have a Just Cause?

Do we ever have a just cause to live in fear? Jairus'
daughter died as Jesus and Jairus were on their way to see
her healed. When Jesus did not reach Jairus' daughter in
time, his faith turned to fear. His only daughter was gone
and the hopelessness that death brings swallowed him up.
Death is final! The fear of loneliness and failure filled his
heart. Is this not a just cause for a father to be afraid?
Jesus did not think so. He turned to Jairus in his grief and
said,

> *'Do not be afraid; only believe, and she will be made
> well.'*[1]

Jairus' fear accepted death, but Jesus' faith confessed her
life.

Mary and Martha had sent a prayer request to Jesus to
come and heal Lazarus. This was a prayer of faith. They
fully expected Jesus to come and heal their brother. Jesus
loved them and they knew it. They were financial partners
sowing into the ministry of Jesus. They had given Him
hospitality on a number of occasions and been His friends
and followers. Why should Jesus not come? But He did

not and Lazarus died. Now all their faith had turned into fear, worry, sorrow and disappointment.

Was this not a just cause for fear? Jesus said **No!** He came with the challenge of, '...*if you would believe you would see the glory of God?'*[2] Even in this extreme case of hopelessness Jesus called them to faith. And just as faith raised Jairus' daughter, so it raised Lazarus. Had they remained in fear, death would have reigned.

When Peter walked on the water and began to sink because he was afraid, did Jesus show him pity? **No!** Jesus rebuked him for his fear and his little faith. All too often we are too soft on unbelief. Jesus constantly rebuked His disciples and the Pharisees for their lack of faith because He knew unbelief was a breeding ground for fear, and fear separates us from truth.

Yes, the storm was intimidating, the seas were life-threatening and the possibility of injury was real. But fear is not the answer – **faith** is! Our relationships may be destructive, they present the possibility of unwanted consequences, yet these are no excuse for failing to believe God.

Jesus was not unloving in His rebukes to Jairus and Peter. He was standing by them. He was also enabling them to face the devastating consequences of their choices. Jesus was holding them responsible for their behaviour while offering the answer to their problems.

For silence to reign where abuse abounds is as much a problem as the situation itself. Fear is not a legitimate cause for avoiding the issue. Jesus says – **only believe!**

## A Servant's Story

Hagar had been the maidservant to Abraham and Sarah for many years. Her employment had been quite a pleasant job over all. Abraham was one of the wealthiest men in the country and was generous of heart towards everyone. She was practically part of the family with the birth of Ishmael. She had experienced a few scraps with Sarah but they had not lasted long. Being so close to the family she was given many privileges and community perks that the other servants never thought of getting.

Her real problems began when Isaac was finally born and Abraham and Sarah were beginning to lavish all their affections, time and money on him rather than on Ishmael. There had always been a tension there but both Sarah and Hagar could cope quite well in spite of it.

Before Isaac was born Hagar had subtle ways of intimidating Sarah, rousing her jealousy over Abraham. Clearly Abraham loved Ishmael and this only poured salt on Sarah's barrenness. Abraham felt the cold war between his wife and Hagar and trusted that when God fulfilled His promise of a son for Sarah's womb the power struggle would end.

It was now Isaac's day. He was given a feast in much celebration. Sarah's heart was proud with joy that God had given her a child in her old age. There was reason for this special feast and lavish display of love. All was well until Sarah noticed Ishmael mocking Isaac. This was intolerable.

The next day Hagar and Ishmael found themselves fired from many years of service, placed on an animal with only a skin of water and a crust of bread, and sent off to wander in the desert. Imagine, after all those years of faithful service all she got was a loaf of bread and water, not even a gold watch. And Abraham was a rich man. She must have felt cheated, used, discarded, abused and angry.

The sun was hot and the sand burning, the water and bread did not last long. And to complicate matters they were lost. Hagar had overstepped her bounds that day and gone too far with her liberties. The seething wounds in Sarah erupted with deadly consequences. Hagar finally realised her pride had got the best of her.

Hagar had been so lost in her thoughts that she failed to notice her son was suffering from dehydration. She quietly pulled him off the animal and put him under a shrub for protection. Now she was afraid. She knew that if they did not find water soon her son and she would die. She panicked and began running around hoping for water. Tears were pouring down her cheeks. She may even have pressed her cheeks next to Ishmael's lips to moisten them from her tears.

It was hard to say how many hours passed before Hagar could no longer take the sight of her son dying. She got up and staggered to another shrub about one hundred metres away. At least there she could not hear her son gasping for water. Watching him die filled her with the horrible realisation that this was all her fault. All she could do was call on the God of Abraham – it was her last hope.

Suddenly an angel appeared to her and said, '*What ails you?*'[3] Those words stunned Hagar: 'What ails me? What do you mean? Does the God of Abraham send me a blind angel? Can he not see what my problem is? My only son is dying. I have lost my job, my security and all my benefits after decades of service. And this angel asks me, what's my problem?'

Like Hagar, many people cry out to God but feel He is blind to their abusive or difficult relationships. 'Why is this angel just standing there? Why does God not change my husband, my wife, friend or employer?' Listen to the words of the angel: *'Fear not...'*[4] Fear was Jairus, Mary and Martha, Peter and Hagar's enemy. Their situations were no excuse for fear, as extreme as they were.

Why were the Israelites afraid of the Babylonians, Jairus of his daughter's death, Peter of the storm and Hagar of her son's death? The answer is found in Isaiah 51:13 *'And you forget the Lord your Maker...'* If we do not know who God is in our life, we will fear death. If we do not believe God is our protection, we will fear the Babylonians. If we do not believe God is our love, we will fear rejection. All fear stems from not knowing and believing who God is!

Why do people remain silent in destructive relationships? They do not know God is Love, God is all in all, God is purpose, God is forgiveness, God is grace, God is victory.

Your situation is no cause for fear, but God is your cause for faith. Freedom comes when we realise we do not have to change people. We must let God change **us**. Facing ourselves is the moment of deliverance. It is not death or storms but the individuals themselves that are the problem. Jesus **confronts** them first, then **addresses** the problem.

### Footnotes

1. Luke 8:50 (NKJV)
2. John 11:40 (NKJV)
3. Genesis 21:17 (NKJV)
4. Genesis 21:17 (NKJV)

# *Chapter 21*

## Time for a Decision

Your life in Christ has ended your relationship with sin:

> *'For he who has died has been freed from sin.'*

Sin still exists and can be appealing, but its ability to dominate us has been nullified. Christ purchased our freedom (Galatians 3:13) and broke the grip of Satan over our lives. Hebrews 2:14 and 15 tells us that Jesus destroyed the Devil, rendered him inoperative, defeated, paralysed, reduced to impotence, dethroned, and unemployed the Devil in regards to our life.

Furthermore, Jesus crucified our self-life, that part of us which was trained to live independently from God. But like sin, self still exists. We still have habits, thought patterns, behaviour responses and memories from the old life.

Sin and self are reality, but we now have a choice to turn a deaf ear to them and walk in the Spirit. Or we can give in to the old urges and lifestyle and walk in the flesh. Paul said,

> *'In a sense you have already passed away, and your life is already firmly united with Christ in God...'*[1]

And again,

> *'When you became one with him, your lower nature was stripped away. That was like being circumcised in Christ's way, and it was a spiritual, not a physical, operation.'*[2]

Jesus Christ removed the old nature from our spirit. He then gave us new life. Our emotions, mind and body however, are still the same, and therein lies the problem. We can choose to live out of our spirits or out of our souls. Romans 8:10 makes this clear:

> *'Your old evil-orientated self is now defunct and the living Spirit within you sensitizes you to what is right and good.'*[3]

This means we do not have to respond with pity, depression, fear, control, self-preservation or with manipulative tactics. That person died. We have a new nature with new life. Neil Anderson writes,

> 'Before we received Christ, we were slaves to sin. But because of Christ's work on the cross, sin's power over us has been broken. Satan has no right of ownership of authority over us. He is a defeated foe, but he is committed to keeping us from realising that. He knows he can block your effectiveness as a Christian if he can deceive you into **believing** that you are nothing but a product of your past, subject to sin,

prone to failure, and controlled by your habits. As long as he can confuse you and blind you with his dark lies, you won't be able to see that the chains which once bound you are broken.'[4]

You are not a victim or an intimidator – they died in Christ. Now is the time to begin **living what you are in Christ**. The Wuest translation of Colossians 3:10 says it this way,

> '... *having stripped off and away from yourselves and for your own advantage the old, antiquated, outworn, decrepit, useless man* [that person you were before you were saved] *with its evil practices, and having clothed yourselves with the new man* [the person you **are** after you are saved].'

Until this fact is believed, it cannot be lived. When we do believe it, the life in us starts flowing out of us. Each day we are to

> '*discover new ways of expressing our new, unique personhood in Christ, ways which are in harmony with who **we really are**.'*[5]

God needs to be seen by the people around us. Choose to

> '*stop assuming an outward expression that does not come from within you and is not representative of what you are in your inner being but is patterned after this age, but change your outward expression to one that comes from within and is representative of your inner being.'*[6]

This choice is a leap of faith. Paul the intimidator took it and learned to keep the old intimidator upon the cross and live out of the newness of life in his inner heart.

God's life on the inside will always cause us to win – the right way, not through intimidation, manipulation, control or false submission. This is the way to win.

> *'Listen, in all things Jesus our great leader has established us as invincible champions through His amazing provision for us. We come out on top every time through Him who set His heart on us.'*[7]

Winning through intimidation, submission, compromise, being a victim of life – these are the world's ways, born out of darkness. Winning through death to self is the way of Christ, born out of the wisdom of grace that makes us more than conquerors.

1.   Repent of old ways.
2.   Believe in the new person God has created you to be.
3.   Face yourself and the problem squarely.
4.   Act upon God's Word regardless of how you feel.
5.   Trust moment by moment.
6.   Run to God, not from the problem.
7.   Choose the way of the Spirit and not the flesh.

This is truth on which we can thrive.

## Footnotes

1.   Colossians 3:3 (Johnson Translation)
2.   Colossians 2:11 (Johnson Translation)
3.   Romans 8:10 (Richert Translation)
4.   The Bondage Breaker – Neil Anderson
5.   Ephesians 4:24 (Johnson Translation)
6.   Romans 12:2 (Wuest Translation)
7.   Romans 8:37 (Richter & Jordan Translation)